Every Petal

a Memory

The Story of a Special Daughter

Every Petal

a Memory

Beth McRobb

Every Petal a Memory

Spiderwize
Remus House
Coltsfoot Drive
Woodston
Peterborough
PE2 9BF

www.spiderwize.com

A CIP catalogue record for this book is available from the British Library.

The views expressed in this work are solely those of the author and do not necessarily reflect the views of the publisher, and the publisher hereby disclaims any responsibility for them.

ISBN: 978-1-911596-08-0

Dedicated to my wonderful daughter, Lesley Hope McRobb,
who made me the person I am
and to my beloved husband, Colin,
whose love gives me strength

If we endeavour to nurture it and allow it to blossom, the
human spirit has the ability to triumph over adversity.

At the end of our lives it is better to have been strengthened by
the memories of the things we did than to have been diminished
by regrets over the things that we didn't.

Beth McRobb, 2016

At the Beginning

If you know there's going to be no happy ending, should you tell the story at all? Does the story have worth without the happy ending?

As I considered the telling of my daughter's story, I had to weigh up these questions in my own mind first and I had to decide whether what I had to say would touch hearts in an uplifting way in spite of the sadness therein. On balance, I think it's a story worthy of the telling, worthy of my lovely Lesley and the life she led – and so though I may not be able to give you a happy ending, I can promise you a remarkable journey.

Colin and I married in 1975. We met when I supported the football team Colin played for – Whitburn Juniors – and when he was side-lined due to a broken ankle we made eye contact a few times and as soon as the plaster was off, Colin asked me out. I was quite literally 'picked up at the bus-stop' after the game one Saturday. I took my young brother, Kenny, to the games and he was most impressed that I was going out with one of the 'stars'. I knew that first night when Colin had given me a run back to college in Hamilton that I had just spent the evening with my soul mate and it didn't take much longer for Colin also to be sure. We were engaged a few months later and married the following year. I had qualified as a Primary School teacher and Colin, who had worked in an analytical laboratory, soon decided that he wanted better prospects and took a job as a Water Treatment Consultant. This took him away to England for months of training which was followed by a successful working life throughout Scotland and beyond. We had been offered a council flat in Whitburn if I would take a teaching job there before we got married but after a couple of years we bought our own home together. I loved teaching but knew that when we had a family I would want to be a stay-at-home Mum for the first few years so we lived quietly and saved all we could with that aim in mind.

Lesley was our much wanted first – and as it turned out, only – child. We had been married for three years and had planned and saved towards the day when we would become parents. A very early miscarriage rocked us but our joy was then the greater when next time the first weeks of pregnancy passed with nothing more than sickness to worry about. We were elated and just couldn't wait for the November due date to come round.

My sickness continued throughout and was later followed by some fainting if I sat in an upright position, but we had no reason to feel worried as the doctors weren't concerned. The baby was growing – it was me who was losing weight - and we counted down the days. In the second half of the nine months I had some niggling feelings that all wasn't well and I tried to talk to Colin about how we would cope if our baby had problems. He told me that it was only natural to have such fears but that nothing would be wrong with our baby – we were clean-living, fit and healthy and I had done everything by the book. What could go wrong? However, the feelings never left me though I kept them to myself and tried hard not to dwell on them.

My due date was November 30th but the week before saw my blood pressure rising too much and it was decided that I should be admitted on the 25th with a view to inducing me. As it turned out, by the time I was in hospital that afternoon, they could tell that I was already in early labour so no intervention was needed. Colin had come in for evening visiting and although I was having some pains, we weren't aware that this was the start of labour and he left for home at 8.00 p.m.

Not long after, the pains increased considerably and the nurses confirmed that I needed to go to the labour room so Colin was phoned to ask him to come straight back to hospital. A long night lay ahead with no one realising that the birth was not going to be straightforward. The last few hours were almost unbearable – I was fully dilated but the baby just couldn't be delivered. Eventually, at 7.55 a.m. on a cold, crisp Sunday, November 26th 1978, our baby daughter was born weighing eight and a half pounds. For a couple of moments Colin was ecstatic and so relieved that she had finally arrived but he quickly sensed the sombre mood in the room and our baby was hurriedly bundled up and taken away rather than given to us. All I could feel was the dreadful sense of my fears being realised but Colin was totally shocked by the reality that there was something very wrong. We were simply told that there were problems and we could tell that members of staff were also shocked. I needed a lot of stitching and Colin was asked to wait outside on his own with no real idea of what was happening. The young female doctor maintained an ominous silence throughout the whole stitching procedure, a silence that spoke volumes. I knew that what lay ahead that day was not going to be easy and I had asked Colin to phone my parents to ask them to come to the hospital.

By the time I had been seen to and Colin was allowed back in with a cup of tea being offered to us both, another doctor had been asked to come to speak to us. He told us that Lesley was an extremely poorly baby and they were very concerned about her chances of survival. She was going to have to be moved to Edinburgh Sick Children's Hospital where more specialised care could be offered. At that point, no one could tell us exactly what was wrong – the doctor on duty had not seen a child with Lesley's problems and could give us no diagnosis or prognosis.

We were in limbo. All they could do was explain that there had obviously been developmental problems in the womb and that Lesley's head, face, shoulders, arms, hands and feet had not formed properly. Even more worryingly, her heart was fibrillating and they weren't sure if there were complete internal blockages or malformed inner tubes.

It was a terrifying picture and almost beyond taking in. Sometime later in the day a senior doctor was called in to see Lesley and explain her condition to us. The diagnosis was Apert's Syndrome, a congenital disorder which loosely means 'fusion of the extremities' and explained all the physical differences which were so apparent. We weren't given lots of information or details – probably because the doctor was telling us all he knew with limited knowledge of a rare syndrome. If the internet had been available, I'm sure we would have pored over computers to try to find out more but all we could do was accept what we were being told and wait to see what happened when she arrived in Edinburgh.

I was most worried that they were going to move her without me having had any time with her and I asked to go to the baby intensive care. They agreed and Colin took me to properly meet our wee daughter. I won't pretend that it wasn't a shock – Lesley had no fingers or toes, just tiny fused hands and feet with a malformed thumb on each hand. Her skull was very obviously misshapen and large, her forehead bulged and her face was simply 'different'. The reasons for her difficult delivery were now very apparent. Colin was stunned and very shaken up and I really couldn't tell what he was thinking or feeling.

Lesley's eyes seemed to completely focus on me when I was allowed to put my hand in through the porthole of the incubator to hold her little hand and stroke her dark hair. They were wise, old eyes, not the eyes of a new born baby, and if the eyes are the windows of the soul, Lesley's soul was a troubled one just then. Yet I adored her from that first touch with a love that was never to weaken or change over the years. At that time, I had quite a strong faith in God and I prayed quietly that if she wasn't going to make it, that she would go gently and quickly without pain or suffering. However, I vowed to her that if she survived, I would always be there for her and that she would experience everything I could give her for as long as she lived.

By this time the nurses had organised for her to be moved and an ambulance was to take her to Edinburgh as quickly as possible. Her incubator already had a tag with the name we had chosen – Lesley - written on it but I told Colin that I had changed my mind about having no middle name. I wanted to add 'Hope' and he readily agreed. This was added to her name label before her journey to our capital city - it was all I could give her as she was taken away from me and it felt like my heart was being ripped out. I was left that afternoon surrounded by the sounds of other people's babies but no precious wee bundle of my own to hold.

Colin, with my Dad accompanying him for support, followed the ambulance at high speed all the way to Edinburgh with lights flashing and sirens blaring. I was left behind with the fear of her not making it and not having her Mum beside her. However, when Colin came back to see me later, I could tell immediately that he too was now besotted with our special baby. He was full of all that had been said and done at 'Sick Kids' hospital and was able to pass on more optimistic news of her chances of survival. He was asked – very bluntly – if 'the mother had rejected the child' and he was able to tell them that nothing could be further from the truth and that I was simply devastated to have been left behind at Bangour Hospital. As soon as that information had been imparted it became obvious that they were pulling out all the stops to help her and she seemed to be holding her own. Our daughter appeared to be a real wee fighter. The first steps of Lesley's journey had been taken and her story had begun.

At that time, it was customary for new mums to stay in hospital with their babies for up to a week but I couldn't bear to be in Bangour, West Lothian when Lesley was in Edinburgh so I asked to be discharged. Colin had already been back to 'Sick Kids' on the Monday morning and the news was better. Lesley's heart had settled down without further intervention, the feared lack of internal passages turned out to have been simply blockages that were clearing and she was breathing well on her own out of the incubator. It seemed almost beyond belief but she was obviously strong enough to fight back from the worst of starts and she had both of us rooting for her. It was wonderful for me to be able to go with Colin for the next trip to the city and for us to be together to support each other. I think that it was then that 'The Three Musketeers' mentality set in for us as a family and that was to endure always.

On arrival it became apparent that Lesley was in the hands of people who cared – a notice had been hung on her cot to say 'Don't bath me, my Mum is coming!' I was deeply touched and couldn't really take in that I was going to be able to hold her and feed her and bath her – what a huge step forward. The wise, troubled look had gone from her eyes and she was simply a very vulnerable wee bundle who needed a lot of love and a Mum and Dad who could be strong for her. She had that aplenty!

I now knew for sure that Colin and I had been able to totally accept this unexpectedly special baby given to our care. Other people's reactions were still to be tested. There had been a split with Colin's family so it was my immediate family's reactions that were most important to us. My parents were obviously shocked and upset on the day of Lesley's birth but it was already apparent that they were completely behind us in our love for our wee daughter and their first grandchild. They had seen her shortly after her birth, my Dad had gone with Colin to Edinburgh and then my Mum had cared for him at night with food and help with the difficult phone calls to break the news to our friends that the birth had brought worries and sadness. I had no doubt that they would accept Lesley and love her but the younger of my two brothers was my big concern.

I had been almost like a second mother to Kenny with twelve years separating us and we were very close. He was also very attached to Colin and often stayed with us after we were married. He was only twelve years old and I really wasn't sure how he would cope with the wee niece we had brought into his world. When he came to 'Sick Kids' with my parents I was very worried about his reactions and about how I would feel if he couldn't cope with Lesley. What a waste of worrying that proved to be! Kenny adored her and was to become her pal rather than her uncle. He said to my parents after that first visit that he could see she had problems, but he just thought she was lovely. Colin and I were so grateful and knew that Lesley would be welcomed into the folds of the family and wrapped in love like a protective blanket.

The days of that first week settled into a pattern of driving in to Edinburgh and spending the day with Lesley, bathing, dressing, feeding and loving her. In our minds we were prepared for this being a long haul before we could have any chance of bringing her home. However, early on the Monday morning the week after Lesley was born we got a phone call from the hospital. I answered and immediately felt rising panic when I realised I was speaking to one of the nurses but she was very quick to reassure me that nothing was wrong. Her next words were a shock – she said she was phoning with a message from Lesley who needed me to bring in her outdoor clothes as she wanted to come home! We just couldn't believe it. Colin had to make a quick trip to Falkirk to collect the pram – I had been superstitious about having it in the house before she was born and we wanted it there for her arrival. Everything else was ready for her and it was with huge excitement that I chose the clothes for her to wear for this momentous day and the cosy wee cocoon carrier that she would slip into for me to hold her in during the journey.

The nurses shared our excitement and the joy was unbelievable – Lesley was coming home and that day we believed anything was possible. What a wee survivor she was and how proud we were of this special baby. My Mum and Dad and Kenny came to visit her that night and for the first time we felt the way other parents would have felt on the birth of their first child. We didn't know what lay ahead, all we knew was that we loved her and she was where she was meant to be. The bond that would see us all through hard times in the years to come had been forged during that first week and we just loved our Lesley.

Major Hurdles

The first weeks were a huge mixture of experiences. No matter how much we wanted to believe that we were just an ordinary family, that was never going to be the case and we had to learn to cope with many aspects of life that we couldn't have been prepared for. Colin had to go back to work as soon as Lesley was at home so in many ways, his life returned to normal. I had to learn to deal with the additional problems that Lesley's condition brought as well as just adapting to being a first time mum. I always liked to think of myself as a coping person and I didn't want to have any feelings of being sorry for myself or feeling stressed. However, Lesley didn't really sleep which was exhausting, and she liked to be held and talked to when she was awake so getting things done was difficult.

Going out with her wasn't that easy either. I had to learn to cope with other people's reactions to my wee daughter. There were people I knew well who crossed the road when they saw me coming with the pram rather than trying to think of what to say. There were others who scarcely knew me at all who made a bee-line for me because they had 'heard that my baby was different and wanted to see her'! Of course there were also lots of lovely people who found just the right thing to say – maybe commenting on her dark hair or the colour of her eyes or the pretty hat she was wearing that her Nana had made for her.

Many, many years later my friend Lynne, who I didn't actually meet till Lesley started Nursery School, told me that she had admired me every time she saw me walking up and down to the shops in our wee town. She had children of her own and she knew that my baby had problems yet I was out with her daily and she was always immaculate in her pram. She had spoken then, without me having any awareness of it, of the courage it must take to just behave like any normal mum. I was quite taken aback and humbled when she told me this and it shows that you never know what impression your example makes on people who are on the periphery of your life. This was something we were to become more aware of in later years.

It was the people in our circle of friends and acquaintances who made the effort to visit us who were most touched by Lesley. One childless, elderly couple we knew, who quite obviously came with a gift because they felt they should, arrived at the door with the lady brusquely saying that they could only stay for five minutes because they were busy. Around three hours later when they were eventually leaving she told me that she had never come across a baby with the magnetism that Lesley had and that she had enjoyed herself more than she could find words to say. These were the magic moments when we knew that it wasn't just us who felt the special qualities our wee lady possessed.

I was introduced to the Health Visitor, Anna Gaul, who was to become someone I trusted and respected and could talk to about the upsetting things that I didn't really want to share with Colin. Anna was very matter of fact and down to earth which suited me just fine. She told us early on that Lesley was lucky to have us as her parents and that though her life would be hard and she would often have her back to the wall, that the wall would always be padded because she had Colin and me behind her. That comment stayed with me and comforted me often when Lesley was having difficult times. Although Anna moved away after a few years, we have always kept in touch and the early care and concern she showed for us all remained constant.

During this time, I had to get used to seeing doctors, nurses, health visitors and making trips to hospital to monitor Lesley's progress. We had to attend Bangour Hospital, where Lesley was born, but we were also referred to the Western General in Edinburgh for regular checks with a consultant. The local appointments at Bangour were just to monitor all the basic health issues, the Edinburgh ones were all focussed on Lesley's head.

It was quite a palaver to get to Bangour even though it was fairly local as it took three buses each way. Once or twice my Mum was able to give me a lift but usually it was a case of hauling everything I would need on and off the bus to get there and back –

and I was often left feeling very frustrated by the end of the visits. The doctor in charge would check basic things like Lesley's hips to make sure that no simple issues had been missed because of the bigger problems. However, although Lesley would be dressed in her prettiest dresses and frilly pants, the doctor would always refer to my wee pink bundle as 'he' and 'him' no matter how often I corrected him. This was in front of nurses and students and I got to dread the visits due to feeling that my baby was just a case number or an interesting, rare condition.

Colin always got time off for the appointments with the consultant so that he could take us to Edinburgh in the car. The consultant told us that there was nothing that could be done to help a child with Apert's Syndrome and that it was just a case of 'wait and see how things develop'. When we asked about the future, he simply told us that nothing was certain. He would examine Lesley at each visit, usually fortnightly, and always measured her skull – but didn't tell us the relevance of this. We asked him where we could get more information on the syndrome and he said that he was arranging for us to see a genetic consultant to discuss our likelihood of having another child affected and that the geneticist might have other information to pass on to us. The result of that visit was that the only book the specialist had been able to get hold of that mentioned Apert's Syndrome was one very bluntly titled 'Degrees of Mental Handicap' which wasn't the most positive information we could be given. How I wish we had been able to turn to Jeeves or Google then!

The geneticist discussed the issues round why Lesley had been born as she was. There were no definite answers for us at that time and we didn't come away feeling particularly reassured about the risks for a second child. It was 'probably' a one off since neither of us had any history of Apert's in our background and we were not carrying a gene that increased the chances. However, there were also no guarantees that it wouldn't happen again and I couldn't help wondering if my very early miscarriage had also been because there were problems. We felt that we simply had to deal with things on a day to day basis and leave bigger decisions for further down the line.

That winter was a very cold one in our area and living high up a hill meant that Lesley and I were pretty much snow-bound at times. In January I was due to go to hospital for my six-week check-up following Lesley's birth and my Mum was going to come to look after Lesley rather than me have to take her on the three buses necessary to get to Bangour. As it turned out, that day the weather was horrendous and Colin came back home having been unable to get to one of his planned appointments and he was in time to take me to the hospital. I didn't really want to go and had been going to phone to say that I wasn't making the journey due to the depth of the snow but Colin was determined that I went. I hadn't stopped bleeding since having Lesley and wasn't sure if this was normal – but I'm very stubborn and hadn't asked anyone in case it appeared that I was making a fuss about myself when I should just have been focussed on Lesley.

However, it turned out that I was right to have been concerned as the doctor found that part of the after-birth had been left behind when Lesley was born – no doubt because of the circumstances at the time – and they then horrified me by saying I would have to come in immediately for a wee operation to put things right. I told them that I wouldn't leave Lesley, but they said that if infection set in I would be of no use to Lesley or anyone else and that there wasn't a choice.

They said that I could come in fasted in the morning and that I would get back home at night, but I was devastated at the thought of leaving my baby and this was a very difficult day for me to handle. As it was, everything was very straightforward and I was home in time to bath Lesley that night. My Mum had gladly looked after her with Kenny able to come too and although she hadn't slept much – as usual – Kenny was very proud to show me that he had discovered that she loved to sit on his knee with her back against his chest facing outwards very contentedly. He was becoming a very proud young uncle and loved to spend time with his wee niece.

As I had said earlier, at that time in my life I had a strong belief in God and Colin and I were both regular church attenders. In the first few very dark days of Lesley's life when it didn't look as though she had much chance of surviving, I had wanted her to be christened. It meant a great deal to me for this to have taken place in case she didn't make it as I felt that her life would have been blessed and her place in the world recognised. However, our minister at that time did not think it was appropriate for this to take place in hospital and he said that we would have to wait till she was at home and could attend the church. If I'm honest, I was very angry about this attitude and felt it was totally wrong, but in those days I was quiet and tended to tip my hat to all officialdom, so we just accepted the decision. My Dad was a church elder in his own church and he had tried speaking to our minister about how we felt, but to no avail.

However, with Lesley at home and thriving, we were able to plan her christening. Janette, my best friend from school days who had also been my bridesmaid, was delighted to be asked to be Godmother – her and her husband Rod had completely accepted Lesley from the beginning and they were always to be 'Aunt Nette and Uncle Rod' to Lesley. It was a day that meant a great deal to all of my family – not least my Gran, who was Lesley's 'Grannie Annie'. They were to develop a very special bond during the early years of Lesley's life and visiting Bonnybridge to see her was almost as special as visiting Harthill to see her Nana and Papa.

Lesley's introduction to Brucefield Church that Sunday morning was to be the start of many happy times at Sunday School and then Brownies and Guides in the church hall. We were the proudest parents ever with Lesley in her beautiful christening gown of white Broderie Anglaise cotton and the magnificent fine wool shawl my Mum had knitted for her. It was lovely to have family and friends back to the house afterwards for a happy celebration. Sometimes the greatest gift was just having an ordinary family gathering in amongst the worries of Lesley's health and future, so we treasured occasions that gave us that joy.

Lesley was more than two months old by now and although she was making progress in lots of ways, she was having hours on end where she cried with obvious pain and thrashed her head continuously from side to side. My Mum thought it could be colic, but although I got some medicine to try, it made no difference. All I could do was hold her but we were frequently both left utterly exhausted by these episodes and it was very upsetting not to be able to help her or ease her suffering. Our trips to the Western General continued but we weren't given any answers to what could be causing Lesley's distress even though I was sure that she had pain in her head.

One day when we went out to visit my Mum and Dad, it was obvious that they had something on their minds. Mum said that they had thought very carefully about whether to tell us about something they had heard but had decided that we needed to have the information. A Harthill lady who had been a nursing matron had attended a conference where one of the speakers had been Ian Jackson, a surgeon at Canniesburn hospital in the west of Scotland. She had taken careful note of what he had to say about his work with children born with craniofacial abnormalities and because she had heard about Lesley's problems, she had made the connection and told my Mum.

My parents didn't want to raise false hopes but the lady was sure that Ian had been talking about Apert's Syndrome in the course of the lecture. We were amazed to find that something could be done to help Lesley and I thought I should phone the consultant at the Western in Edinburgh to let him know what we had heard. I told him what we knew and mentioned Ian Jackson by name, but he said that nothing at all could be done for Lesley and reiterated what he had been saying regularly that in our case it was just a case of waiting to see how she developed. I trusted in his knowledge and believed him but was sad to realise that our wee glimmer of hope had very quickly died.

However, Colin, doting Dad and not quite such a trusting person as me, was not accepting of what I had been told. He came home a couple of days later looking a bit sheepish and told me that he had done something that I might not approve of. He had been working in the Glasgow area and had decided to drive to Canniesburn. On arrival, he had explained at the reception desk why he was there looking for information about Ian Jackson's work – and remarkably he was able to speak to Marjory, Ian's wife who was in the building. She confirmed then and there that Ian did work with children with the kind of problems Lesley had and she said that she would get him to phone us late that night when he got home. Indeed, she herself phoned me in the early evening and told me more in one phone call about Apert's Syndrome than we had been told in all the visits to Edinburgh. I couldn't believe what I was hearing or that Colin had been so right not to accept what I had been told earlier.

Ian did phone as soon as he got home very late that night and having asked various questions, he told us that there was no time to waste in getting Lesley in to see him. He told us that we would need to go to our G.P. and ask for a second opinion on Lesley's care and have her referred to him. He stressed that we needed to do this urgently and that we should let our doctor know this so that no time was wasted in referrals being made. He promised that as soon as he got the referral, he would arrange an appointment for us to meet with him and Mr. Rab Hyde, the neuro-surgeon from the Southern General Hospital in Glasgow who was part of his team.

I was able to speak to our doctor who it turned out had worked with Ian Jackson at one time in Falkirk and who was a great admirer of his work. She agreed to send the referral immediately and everything was set in motion that day. We had to go back to the Western at the end of that week for our routine visit, and as always, the consultant was taking the measuring tape out of the drawer by the time we had sat down. He began noting the measurements and we said that we needed to tell him what had happened over the course of the last week since the phone discussion I had had with him.

When we told him that we had spoken with Ian Jackson and that we had asked for a referral to him for a second opinion, he put the measuring tape back in the drawer, closed Lesley's file and said that we should leave and not bother making an appointment to come back to see him. We were shocked and I was upset because he was obviously greatly annoyed by what we had done. However, we learned later that many doctors did not agree with Ian's pioneering surgery and disapproved of the sort of major work that would be entailed if he decided to work with a child such as Lesley where there would be no guarantees of any success. With the benefit of age and life experience, I can fully appreciate the beliefs of doctors such as the consultant in Edinburgh, but that does not excuse him in my mind for not telling us that interventions were possible or that there were people who knew more about Apert's Syndrome than him. We had been asking him questions, we were obviously caring parents and we desperately wanted to feel that we were doing our best for our wee girl. I think at the very least that he should have been more honest with us when I phoned to discuss what we had heard. However, at the time we simply pinned our hopes on what Ian would say when we met him and he examined Lesley.

That day came very quickly and it was quite a traumatic one for us. We arrived at Canniesburn Hospital not quite sure what to expect and not sure whether to be scared or optimistic. We had just turned 25 and 27 years old by now and would both have considered ourselves to be quite mature anyway. I was only twenty when I started teaching and was aware that many of the parents would think I was very young, so it had been important for me to present as a mature, sensible, capable and caring person who was fit to have their children in my charge. Colin's job had meant months living away from home during training, long hours on the road and coping with huge amounts of nightly paperwork on top of long days where he had to deal with everyone from boiler men to directors of wide ranging companies.

However, the growing up we had done in the last three months topped all the rest of our life experiences to date and we needed every ounce of maturity to cope with the next couple of hours in the examination room. There seemed to be dozens of people present or dipping in and out, squeezed in to a small area and all totally focussed on the wee pink bundle in my arms. Colin was relegated to standing out at the door as there simply wasn't any space for him and I was only in the room because I was holding Lesley. It was obvious at that point that our feelings were the lowest priority and that everyone was hanging on Ian Jackson's words – us included. It was terrifying and reassuring in equal measures and very difficult to handle at first.

Ian gained almost celebrity status a little later because of the reconstruction work he did for David, the boy from Peru who was to become the adopted son of him and Marjory with David's story being told in a series of television documentaries by Desmond Wilcox. That day we saw first-hand what made him such a special man and surgeon. He had focus, single-mindedness and courage to say and do what he believed was required and the vision to determine what was possible.

We quickly realised that major surgery on a scale out-with our experience was being discussed and that there was some urgency in this. Although I was right in the middle of the room holding Lesley, very little was said to me during the examination with just a series of questions to be answered at times in the middle of the discussions within the team. However, we did gather that lots of x-rays and photographs were required and then the planning of the reconstruction of Lesley's skull could take place. Eventually Colin and I became the focus of the discussions and many of the team left the room. Ian explained that the surgery would take anything from ten to fourteen hours to perform and that there were huge risks involved. He also mentioned hydrocephalous for the first time and explained that this fluid on the brain was a possibility and this actually explained the Edinburgh doctor's constant measurements of Lesley's head – large build-ups of fluid would have enlarged her skull further and confirmed the presence of the condition that Ian suspected.

The extreme bouts of crying and head thrashing that I told them about were thought to be signs that Lesley's brain was already being affected by the fact that her skull bones were like a rigid band round her brain and brain growth would mean crushing. Unlike other babies, there were no normal 'soft-spots' or fontanelles another factor in the difficult birth, but Lesley's soft bulging forehead was not protecting her either. Indeed, she must have been really suffering terrible pain at this time because the hours of crying and head thrashing stopped from the day of the first operation and never recurred.

I won't be too graphic in my descriptions of the planned operation but she would have to be cut from ear to ear up over her skull and her face would be 'removed' while her skull was restructured. We could hardly take in what we were hearing. Nowadays there are many television programmes dealing with major surgery but at that time in the seventies we were utterly naive as to what lay ahead. I kept thinking about the risks and about whether my baby could possible withstand all that was being planned. I remember Colin asking Ian what he would do if it was his daughter and he said that he really couldn't give a personal response to that – but Rab Hyde said that we had very little choice. It was obvious that without the operation Lesley would either die or have a very painful deterioration as her brain was damaged as it grew. What choice indeed. We agreed that she had to be given the best chance of survival and the operation was on.

Time was of the essence and the necessary photographs and x-rays were taken to allow detailed plans to be developed in advance of the surgery and within a very short time we had a date for Lesley's admission to the Southern General Neurological Unit at around four and a half months old. On looking back, I sometimes wonder how we coped but then Lesley was always at the centre of everything and we just did what was necessary on a daily basis to support her.

On the day of the operation they told us that it would be better if we just stayed at home – there was nothing we could do for her and it would be a very long day. However, we quickly realised that being over 30 miles away from our baby when she was undergoing such drastic surgery was simply not an option for us. Colin had taken the day off work anyway and we decided that we had to be in the hospital so we headed through to Govan to be closer to her.

At some point in the day, we picked up on the fact that there were surgeons from all over the world who had come to be in the viewing gallery and that this was no ordinary operation. The doctors must have been told that we were in the building because later on we were given some updates on progress and reassured that all was going according to plan. The operation had started early in the morning but it was after 6.30 in the evening before Mr Jackson and Mr Hyde were able to come and tell us that the rest of the team were finishing off the procedure and that Lesley was as well as could be expected at that point. They were careful to make sure we knew that the next few days were crucial and that she wasn't out of the woods yet.

All we wanted was to see her and touch her but we had to wait a while before she was ready to be taken to intensive care and what a sight was waiting for us there. Her swaddled head seemed larger than the rest of her wee body lying in the cot and she was just so vulnerable. She was hooked up to all sorts so a cuddle was simply out of the question but we were able to sit with her and reach in and touch her and hold her hand – and hope that she knew how much we loved her. There was no way we could leave the hospital with Lesley in such a critical state and we were most grateful late that night when we were told that there was a 'bed in a wardrobe' in one of the offices and that we could stay there and get some rest while still being on hand if she needed us. It was explained clearly to us – almost too clearly – that the next 24 hours was crucial and that we could lose her at any minute. This was a dreadful shock for us because we had innocently thought that if she came through the initial surgery our worst worries would be over. When we reluctantly left her side in the early hours of the morning to try to get some rest we went to the office where the bed was being provided. I don't think either of us will ever forget lying there, unable to sleep, unable to voice our fears and listening to the wall clock which ticked away the seconds and gave a little juddering hiccup as it passed every minute. We stayed there over the weekend too until we were more sure that she was stable enough for Colin to go to work and me to go home at night.

There were no facilities at that time for parents to stay with their children but we were most welcome from crack of dawn till late at night in the intensive care unit. We were treated with real care and affection and got cups of tea and slices of toast at various times. I remember Colin being brought a radio to listen to the football results and it was wee touches like this that made it more bearable as it certainly wasn't an easy situation to be in. Colin and I have always been best friends and soul-mates as well as husband and wife and our closeness enabled us to cope with it all. I remember a staff nurse telling us that she knew we would always be a strong partnership because of what she saw in us over the space of that first couple of weeks. She said she had noted that we were a real team and a tight unit in a situation in which they often saw widening cracks in relationships and families being driven apart. Neurological intensive care is a very difficult place to spend time in for patients and for their families. Every case there is a very serious one.

The General Election was held in May that year when Margaret Thatcher came to power and Lesley was still in intensive care. She hadn't been able to sleep that night and the nurses said that they thought she was a wee Tory who wanted to hear the results coming in throughout the night! Lesley couldn't actually have been less interested in politics by the time she could have voted but the early signs didn't show that.

The first crucial time passed and after a week or two Lesley was able to be moved to the children's neurological ward. Everyone was commenting on how much better Lesley was looking than before the operation – Colin, my parents, nurses, doctors, all were raving about the difference the surgery and restructuring had made. I was very quiet when all this talk was going on around me because I truly didn't see much difference and nothing that justified what my baby had been put through. The only person who picked up on my silence was Ian Jackson who still came over from Canniesburn regularly to see Lesley and monitor her progress. He must have realised, maybe from past experience, that through my 'rose coloured mother-love glasses' I had always thought my daughter was lovely and I just felt the same way. He came into Lesley's room one afternoon carrying a small case. He signalled for me to come over to the window, which I did, and he took one photographic slide after another from the case and held them up to the light for me to look at. They were the ones that had been taken at Canniesburn before the operation and were the most candid, cruel shots, taken from every angle to show the extent of Lesley's head and face problems. Not a word was said between us but silent tears poured down my face as I realised for the first time what everyone else had been seeing – my baby was so much improved that it was beyond belief. Ian put the slides back in the case, patted my shoulder and left – and it was then that he gained god-like status in my eyes.

However, it wasn't all good news as the worry about hydrocephalous proved correct. We were told that surgery would be needed to fit a shunt to drain the fluid to her abdomen but that time was needed to allow the newly reconstructed skull to start to knit together before a further operation. There were sad days ahead – if Lesley was lying down to allow the skull and new forehead a chance to settle, fluid was leaking out of the stitch line across her head. If she was put into a wee cradle chair in a sitting position to help this, her forehead was dropping down over her eyes.

It's unbearably hard to see such things happening to your baby and not to be able to do a thing about it. However, there was never a choice, we simply had to deal with what each day brought. I think Colin and I became quite institutionalised in the weeks and months of that first year. Colin would take me and drop me off in Govan around 6.30 every morning and then drive all over Scotland in the course of his working day before returning at night to have a meal with me in the hospital canteen. Things were much stricter in the ward and we had to leave at 7.30 in the evening no matter how Lesley was. She might have been asleep since Colin's arrival and only awake for a matter of minutes but we still had to leave on the bell. Initially I hadn't been allowed into the ward till 10.30 in the morning but one of the doctors saw me sitting in the open area outside the lifts one day and asked why I was there. I explained that Colin had to drop me off before going to work as public transport took hours from Whitburn and he then arranged for me to be allowed in as soon as I arrived which was brilliant. I still had to go out over lunchtime regardless of how Lesley was but we put up with everything we had to, just to be with her whenever possible.

Colin's paperwork had to be done when we arrived home at night and he also took work in to the hospital to do at the weekend. In those days there were no automatic washing machines so my time at home was spent answering phone calls about Lesley and trying to keep on top of washing, drying and ironing. The only shopping required was for bread, milk and cereals to cope with breakfasts and Colin's packed lunches as main meals were all in the hospital canteen. It was a difficult, regimented way of life but thankfully we were both in complete agreement that it was the way we wanted it to be for Lesley's sake.

After a few weeks in the ward, the shunt operation was deemed to be possible so we prepared ourselves again for what that would bring. Colin didn't feel he could take any more time off work and it was with great reluctance that he left me on my own at the hospital on the day of the operation. I doubt if people realised the strain he was under during this time, trying to do his job and keep on top of all that was involved with it and also making sure that I got to the hospital every day. I remember once having his boss's wife telling me on the phone that she had been in the office when Colin called in and that she thought he was looking tired and could do with a holiday. I was speechless! I had to tell her that he had been using his holidays on days when things were really bad for Lesley and that we had no way of knowing how often that would happen in the days to come. There wasn't the sort of compassionate leave that might be built into contracts of employment nowadays for the parent of a disabled child and Colin took his job very seriously. His boss, who Colin greatly admired and respected, eventually said to him that if he could justify it to himself to take time off, then it was all right for him to do so – but with the work ethic and commitment that Colin had, that simply meant that he was even less likely to say he needed to take time off!

Quite innocently we thought that as soon as the shunt was fitted all would be well and Lesley would get home. However, we hadn't known then that shunts could block or get infected or have adhesions form which all led to them having to be replaced. She would have a shunt fitted, recover from the surgery and then begin to deteriorate and the shunt would have to come out again due to a blockage or an infection. It wasn't just a case of taking one out and putting another one in at the same time. If there was any infection that had to be completely clear before risking a new shunt going in so weeks and weeks passed without her being much further on.

One beautiful early summer Saturday, Mr Hyde came in to see her at the weekend which he often did if she was poorly. I think he must just have felt very sorry for us, sitting inside when the rest of the world was enjoying sunny warmth. He came back into her room to say that he thought we should all get out and have some fresh air and we were stunned. Till this point, it had been deemed best that Lesley just wore baby clothes belonging to the hospital to make laundry and safe-keeping easier. Mr Hyde didn't want her going out without a hat either and he also wanted her in a pram rather than being carried. The next hour or so was spent with the staff trying to come up with solutions to the obstacles. A horrible yellow and orange Paisley patterned pram from the toy cupboard was cleaned and the mop-cap type hat from the Holly-Hobby doll who usually occupied the pram was washed and dried and called in to service. A hospital blanket completed the look.

We must have seemed the strangest family ever but we were overjoyed to be out walking through Govan – a fairly smartly dressed young couple with a hideous pram and an oddly dressed baby - but it just didn't matter to us what anyone thought! The next day, when we had to go out at lunchtime we passed on a visit to the canteen and drove to Paisley following directions from one of the nurses to get to a superstore where we would easily get some summer baby clothes and wee cotton hats. Never again did we want to take our precious baby out looking the way she did that Saturday and we kept a supply of clothes in her room from then on just in case we got the opportunity to 'escape' from the ward. In years to come she had a constant supply of beautiful crocheted and knitted hats all made by her Nana to fit her perfectly. Her head size and shape didn't conform to normal patterns but my Mum was always able to adapt patterns so that the hats fitted perfectly and she soon found the styles that best suited Lesley as well as keeping her warm. Wee mitts would also be made to measure so trips out on bright, cold winter days didn't ever trouble Lesley. However, there will always be a place in my heart for the Holly-Hobby hat for that first trip out of hospital!

Holding on ... Just

At one point during that summer of 1979, when Lesley was without a shunt and waiting till she was well enough for the next operation to fit a new one, Mr Hyde said that she could go home for the weekend – amazing! He said that from late Friday afternoon till Sunday night we could all be together in our own house and we were so excited about it. Colin came straight from work to collect us and we were stunned when we stepped into the living room and Lesley began pointing to things and smiling in recognition – she really seemed to remember her own home which moved us greatly.

We had a lovely time on the Friday night and having Lesley in her own cot when we went to bed was wonderful. Our plans for the weekend were to take her visiting her grandparents and uncle and just to enjoy relaxing at home. However, it didn't work out as we had planned. Lesley had slept on and off during the night and Saturday morning started well with us all enjoying having breakfast together. Colin and I got ready for going out and then as I was changing Lesley's nappy on my knee she made a very strange noise and went completely limp in my arms. We realised that she had stopped breathing and was beginning to turn blue and I screamed at Colin to phone for an ambulance. As he was doing so, he was shouting to me that we didn't have time and that I would have to do mouth to mouth. I had some first aid training and hoped that I was doing the right thing and Colin was relaying this to the person who answered his call. After what seemed like an eternity but was actually a very short time, Lesley gave another strange sound and gasped for breath – we had her back with us and she quickly began to 'pink up' again. On being questioned on the phone, Colin had explained that she was just home for the weekend and we were immediately advised to take her straight back to hospital.

We hurried there and explained what had happened but it was very obvious that they thought we had just panicked about the responsibility of having her at home and we were rather patronisingly told to sit in the day room till her cot was ready. Just after we settled there, exactly the same thing happened again and suddenly there was a very different attitude with Lesley being rushed away and doctors being sent for. These attacks continued for the rest of the day though they lessened in their intensity. It turned out to be a form of epilepsy caused by imbalance in the brain after the operations. She had to be put on two different medications to control it though by the time she was three years old she was stable enough to be weaned off the medicine. It was a reminder of how vulnerable our wee daughter was in spite of the progress she was making.

The shunt situation took till the December of that year to be fully resolved with four attempts being required before she had a working, uninfected one in place and we had some scary times when Lesley was very poorly. It meant removing blocked or infected shunts and then waiting for her to be well enough to try to replace them. At one point in the autumn when yet another one had needed to be removed due to adhesions, Mr Hyde was happy enough with her general health to decide that she could have some time at home. She wasn't formally discharged but we did get some weeks in our own home while she recovered from the removal operation and could be sure to be infection free.

The medication needed to be increased a bit as she grew. I had another frightening episode as I walked home with her in her buggy one day and she had another loss of consciousness though she was breathing. However, considering her growth rate, I was reassured to be told that it was a simple case of increasing the dosage to keep her stable. During this time Lesley was loving life at home and her appetite and enjoyment of home-cooked food was wonderful. In the ward, when she was just being bottle-fed, life was simple, but when I was trying to wean her onto solids it was more difficult.

Usually it was a case of hoping there was soup on the menu for one meal and maybe potatoes with gravy from a meat dish for another. We bought her yoghurts to keep in the fridge in the ward kitchen but she was rather limited in what was on offer. She quickly progressed to such things as mince with vegetables and in all honesty, she turned down nothing! In later years Lesley always loved food and would eat anything whilst still appreciating the finer delicacies offered to her on a menu if we ate out and I'm sure that this love of all things edible started in those first days when it really was a case of 'take it or leave it'.

Her appetite was always apparent and I can remember a time when she had just had one of the shunt operations and the only place left for the drip line to be inserted was her ankle. When she should have been lying sleeping in her cot to recover she was almost pulling the drip out with the amount of kicking she was doing as she howled at the top of her voice. The nurses were concerned that she was in pain but I was sure it was simply that she was starving and asked if she could have some milk. They were very reluctant for her to have anything too quickly in case it made her sick but eventually agreed that I could try feeding her to see what happened. It took all of two seconds for the crying – and the kicking – to stop and our hungry wee lady was easily satisfied and relaxed enough to get some sleep.

This hunger level came in very handy on another occasion when she had been poorly and needed a brain scan. It was essential that she was lying on her back and keeping her head completely still but her chest was bad and an anaesthetic was out of the question. The doctors asked me how I felt about letting her go past feeding time so that she was very hungry and then taking her down to the scanner and feeding her while she was lying in the drum. I was happy to give it a go and the timings were worked out in advance. I had a bottle ready to take with us and Lesley was desperate for it by the time we went to the scanner. When I lay her down, the technicians were ready and I began to feed her. The only movement was her lips as she sucked furiously on the bottle and I could only cross my fingers that the scan was taking place successfully. Just as I became aware that we were down to the last wee drop of milk, I got the thumbs up – it had been timed to perfection and the scan results were as clear as they would have been under total sedation.

Back at home we were discovering the down-side to Lesley's mal-formed respiratory tubes – croup became a constant problem for her and we spent many hours steaming her to try to relieve the effort to breathe. She had frequent chest infections to cope with too and was on antibiotics for at least half of each month. Just when it had been decided that she couldn't wait any longer for another attempt to fit a shunt, she had another chest infection. We were in hospital and the fluid pressure in her brain was worryingly high so the shunt was needed urgently. This was just before her first birthday and the doctors had difficult choices to make. General anaesthetic with a chest infection and Lesley's poor breathing was very risky but she just couldn't wait for a new shunt to relieve the pressure and the operation had to go ahead.

She came through the surgery and ironically this turned out to be the shunt that didn't get blocked or infected and actually was able to be left in thereafter. However, she was not a well wee soul and had to be wrapped up in foil as she was going into shock.

Lesley's general condition was very quickly deteriorating and I was becoming increasingly worried about her. Being in a neurological ward tended to mean that the focus was all on heads but when Lesley felt burning hot the next morning and stopped wanting to eat or drink I asked for her to be checked more thoroughly. I was meant to be reassured that although her temperature turned out to be well over 100 degrees, that was probably because of the heat in the room and the fact that she had already had a cold.

When Colin came in after his work that day, he shared my concerns that she was far from well but no one else seemed to be at all concerned and we had to leave as usual when the bell rang at 7.30 p.m. When I went in the next morning she was worse and I told nurses that I was really worried. Over the course of the day, no matter what I did, I couldn't get Lesley to open her eyes or feed and she became unresponsive to my voice or even little nips to try to rouse her. Her nappy remained bone dry and again I tried to point this out to the nursing staff with no reaction other than to say that her shunt wound was healing nicely.

I'm usually a very calm and strong person in a crisis but by the time Colin arrived that evening and came into the room I totally broke down and sobbed in his arms as I told him that I thought our baby was dying. Colin was shocked and knew that I wouldn't be reacting like this unless I was really worried – I had coped with everything else that had been thrown at me during that long, hard year and now I was broken. He went out and demanded that a doctor be sent for to examine Lesley thoroughly and was told that the doctors had looked at her head that morning and been happy with the wound and the functioning of the shunt. Colin said that we wanted a paediatrician to see her from the main hospital and that we would not be leaving until we knew what was wrong.

When 7.30 p.m. came that night we just kept our heads down and stayed by Lesley's side in the wee single room. One of the nurses came in after a few minutes to ask us if we hadn't heard the bell and to remind us that we needed to leave. I said that we were not going anywhere until the doctor had seen Lesley and we were told that this could take a while. We said that we would be there for as long as it took and she left obviously unhappy with our attitude. Sometime later, a doctor arrived and very quickly told us that our baby had double pneumonia and was very ill indeed. Her shunt might be fine but nothing else was! She was prescribed medication and emergency physiotherapy on her chest was organised to be started immediately to try to relieve the congestion. Lesley hated the pounding of the physiotherapy over the next days and her spirit seemed to be diminished. No matter how hard we tried to entertain her, neither her Dad nor I could get a smile from her and the same was true when her grandparents and Kenny came to visit. Then one night her Uncle Pete, who had never previously visited, popped in to see her. He approached her cot, prodded her with his finger and said 'Hi' and Lesley beamed a beautiful smile of response. I didn't know whether to be delighted to see her smiling or furious that she had saved this precious moment for my brother rather than me! Thankfully her usual bright cheerfulness had returned to us and the physiotherapy coupled with the correct medication, had her beginning to recover within days.

The day of her first birthday came around and although she was still quite poorly, she was well enough to enjoy a wee party in the ward. We hadn't expected anything to be allowed because although it was the children's ward of the neurological unit, it was run more as an adult ward and it was not like being in a children's hospital. I made a cake the night before but staff had also organised a cake and some party food to come up from the kitchens so that everyone could join in the special occasion. Lesley had the afternoon party with her doctors in attendance as well as the nurses and other children – and then another celebration at night with her Nana and Papa and Uncle Kenny. We could scarcely believe the difference a week had made but often wondered what might have happened if we had waited another day before demanding attention for our wee ill daughter.

Incredibly, just a few days later during the first week of December we got the news we had been waiting for throughout the year – Lesley could be discharged! I can't even begin to look for the words to tell you how that made us feel. She had a shunt that was working, the wounds were healing and her chest was clearing. We could look forward to her hair growing in again without a further operation being imminent - and the surprise was that there was blonde hair now and not the dark hair she had been born with

- and most importantly, we could all be at home. The days of being institutionalised were over and we could be a real family again looking forward to Christmas together.

A week or so before Christmas Colin's company had organised a weekend in Aviemore for the team and their families, something we had not thought for a moment that we could attend, but with the news of the discharge and the functioning shunt report, we decided that we would go up for an overnight. Lesley had not totally recovered from the pneumonia and still tired easily and her wee shaved head was covered in pretty horrific scars but we were able to watch her with the other children having a lovely time at the children's tea on the afternoon we arrived. We had not had many such happy experiences due to the trials of this first year of Lesley's life but I think it just made the moment more precious and more highly valued by us. One thing was certain - every minute of every difficult day that we had been through was worth it to see Lesley enjoying herself and we just adored her and admired her spirit and love of life. Never once had we thought of having a day away from the hospital and Colin had worked very hard to keep on top of his job while still being there for Lesley and for me. We were 'The Three Musketeers' and that was to be how we always thought of ourselves in the years to come.

Christmas that year was just wonderful. Colin had time off work and we could relax and enjoy family life. Lesley obviously didn't know what it was all about but loved the sense of occasion and the Christmas dinner with all the family around her in her own house. I think we could have saved ourselves money on presents because she spent most time with the wrapping paper and the plastic box that her wee slippers had been in, but we were just overjoyed to be having fun with her. Maybe this was our first indication that our wee daughter was to grow to be the least materialistic person you would ever meet. She had a lovely new red and white dress which made her look very festive and when she got her hands on a chocolate covered honeycomb bar that night, her delight was boundless. Her wee hands couldn't hold it easily and with no teeth she couldn't bite it, but that didn't stop the pleasure. She simply sucked it till she had conquered it and the red and white dress ended up completely brown – but the chocolate framed smile was the best Christmas present ever for Colin and me.

Things Looking Up

New Year's Eve made us reflect on all that had happened in 1979 and be very grateful for the fact that Lesley had come through so much to give her the chance of having some quality of life. At midnight, we took a glass of wine each up to Lesley's room and stood beside her cot. She was sound asleep and very peaceful with slow steady breathing that was a joy to listen to. We each touched her as we raised our glass in a toast to 1980 – hopefully an easier year for our precious wee bundle and it felt as if this was a fresh start with more optimism than we could have had the year before.

Settling into normal family life was great and the mundane things like shopping and cooking and cleaning were a pleasure – most of the time anyway! Lesley's general health was still badly affected by croup and with our area being cold, damp and often foggy in winter months, there was a lot of time that we had to spend indoors. Many hours were spent in the kitchen with pots and kettles boiling to create a steamy atmosphere to give her chest a wee bit of relief. Colin often came home at night from wherever he had been in the country that day to tell us that within a few miles in any direction we would have been enjoying better weather, but that was just how it had to be. The highlight of our week tended to be a trip to Woolco department store in Livingston at the weekend to do our shopping and enjoy a cuppa together. This must have set a pattern of pleasure because Lesley always looked forward to a wee run in the car with a hot chocolate waiting for her somewhere.

She also loved visits to Harthill to see her Nana and Papa and trips through to Bonnybridge to see her Great Gran – or Grannie Annie as she called her. At my parents' house, pots and pot lids were a big attraction in spite of there being a selection of toys kept for Lesley to enjoy during visits there. My Gran always greeted us on arrival with a cry of 'Oh my baby' as she reached out to take Lesley and they had a really lovely relationship for the first few years of Lesley's life until my Gran died. There was a tall larder unit cupboard in Gran's kitchen – the heart of the home where we always sat to have a cuppa and a chat – and Lesley soon discovered that the bottom doors of the unit opened very easily. Inside were all Gran's baking ingredients stored in tall, cylindrical tins that weighed a ton. Lesley loved to haul all of them out, to my dismay but Gran's delight. I was always worried that one would get knocked over and flour or sugar would spill everywhere but Gran just didn't care. She was so amazed at the power in Lesley's tiny wee hands and her determination to succeed in her task against all odds.

That determination became apparent in other ways. I found Lesley in the middle of my carpet-tiled kitchen floor one day with an empty bottle of blackcurrant cordial in a pool all around her. It was a screw-top bottle and I couldn't understand how Lesley had managed to open it with the hand problems she had. When I asked her to show me what she had done to get it open, she anchored the upright bottle between her knees using them like a vice and then she used the flat of both hands to work away at the lid until she got it to turn. This was an amazing achievement which so filled me with pride that I congratulated Lesley rather than giving her a row for the mess she had created!

Such celebrations had to be carefully handled though. When Lesley was born, her hands were not just fused, they were tiny and the little misshapen thumb she had was tight against the main part of her hand with no movement. She had a teething ring with coloured plastic key shapes hanging from it and I began to force a key into her hand to encourage her to feel it and move her thumb. When that gained success and I realised that I could do more to encourage movement through sensation I tried putting strips of greaseproof paper in her hand so that if she moved her thumb she would feel it and hear it crinkling. This worked really well and soon Lesley was enjoying the success of crushing and eventually tearing the paper. Again I congratulated her enthusiastically, desperate for Colin to get home to show off the latest achievement. However, for Lesley, paper was paper – and the daily newspaper ended up having to be hidden on the top of a unit to stop it suffering the same fate as the greaseproof paper strips!

Lesley liked a lot of stimulation and demanded my attention unless I was obviously busy. Sitting down to relax with a quiet cuppa was not a luxury I enjoyed often and when work was complete, Lesley expected my full involvement with her. Getting a baby walker helped a bit although trying to stop her running to touch the radiators was a constant battle – until the day I didn't get there in time to stop a wee hand making very hot contact. Not a cry or whimper escaped Lesley's lips – but she didn't ever go near them after that. Another entertaining addition to the toys in the house was a baby bouncer which hung from the kitchen doorway with Lesley securely supported in it and able to make it bounce up and down by her own efforts. She loved it and would happily bounce long enough for me to have a coffee. This lasted until the night she was in it when my Dad arrived and he turned it into a swing which was obviously much more fun than just gently bouncing – and from then on, only swinging was entertaining enough for my fun-loving daughter.

We also enjoyed lots of 'Sunday lunch' visits with friends, some who also had their own children by then, others who didn't. One of Lesley's favourite visits was to see her Aunt Nette and Uncle Rod and a lot of that was to do with the fact that Rod liked to 'help' her to play with anything the least bit technical or constructional that she had taken with her. I well remember a time when Lego was her favourite toy and she took her box with her. This was before the days when Lego had moving parts and a wheel was the extent of the technology. This didn't stop Rod being able to create a magnificent working carousel-type structure with moving parts which Lesley was itching to get her hands on – but that she had to wait to play with until Uncle Rod had it all perfected to his high standards.

Our Health Visitor, Anna, told me that I needed to make sure that Lesley got to enjoy the company of other children and that I should consider joining a mother and toddler club. I'm not really a 'join a club' type of person but I saw the wisdom in Anna's advice and always wanted to do what was best for Lesley. So, with my innate shyness held in check, we headed to Murraysgate at the west end of Whitburn for our first taste of mum and baby socialising. No matter how confident I tried to appear, it was really hard to walk in to an established group and not be sure of the kind of welcome we would receive. However, my fears proved groundless and we were accepted and welcomed into the company and Lesley was immediately crawling around enjoying herself. This was where she learned about other children, about sharing and standing her ground, about noise, tears and laughter and she simply thrived on it. I got to look forward to our Monday visits and I think we both got a lot out of the experiences over the years and we continued to go until Lesley started nursery school.

Routines were developed and the difficult first year was fading to a memory. We would get the bus to Harthill every week to visit her Nana who returned the visit to us on another day weekly. Her Papa came out one evening a week to enjoy bath-time with ducks and wind-up bath toys, singing to her and generally having fun. We visited friends and they visited us. We had days out doing simple family things with me remaining determined to keep my promise about Lesley getting to experience everything that it was in my power to give her. When the modernised Glasgow Underground re-opened in spring 1980, we were there to ride the circuit just because it was an adventure we could share as a family. I'm sure that the seventeen-month old bundle on my knee couldn't really have cared less about the trip but she did beam and smile at everyone around her and we had a great day out. Simple trips like this were often to give us pleasure and over the years they grew into bigger journeys – but probably that early adventure symbolised the promise to give Lesley as many experiences and opportunities as possible and the joy was to be doing happy family things together.

Colin continued to work hard, putting in long hours both out in the field and at home in the office but he was gaining respect and achieving success in his job. The hardest bits were him needing to go to England for meetings or courses but we coped with it. I remember the first time he had to be away for a whole week after Lesley was home from the hospital. He missed her terribly and phoned every night – there were no mobiles in those days so he had to wait till he was finished for the day and find a phone to use. He was counting the hours till he would get home to both of us and hating the fact that he was away for longer than just a couple of days.

Having been away since the Sunday, he got finished early enough on the Friday to be home before Lesley went to bed. When I heard him, I hurried to welcome him and after a quick hug for me, he rushed to the living room expecting an excited greeting from his beloved daughter. Lesley glanced up briefly and then just returned to what she had been doing. Colin was totally devastated to think that she hadn't been missing him but it was simply that for her there hadn't been a great deal of difference between his long working days and nights spent in the home office and she just didn't react. However, as she got a wee bit older, she grew to hate him being away and never again did he get a lukewarm welcome home from a journey south.

Just after the trip on the underground, we were asked to go back for tests and assessments to the Southern General hospital and I dreaded the thought of the long hospital days and the possibility of finding that there were problems requiring intervention. It was lovely to see everyone again and it turned out to be just a quick week of general checks to confirm that all was well. Mr Hyde was a believer in 'if it ain't broke, don't fix it' and we were home again by the weekend with just a six-month outpatient appointment pencilled in. This felt like a huge step forward and we were able to relax and look ahead

We decided that it would be great to have a holiday and I booked a caravan in Whitley Bay for early summer. We had checked to see if we could have one with a cot and were delighted to be allocated one with a single bed that had a cot side. Lesley was eighteen months old by this time and although she wasn't walking on her own, she was getting around well if she had something to hold onto. The caravan suited her perfectly as she could get around the whole of it on her own two feet with no help from us.

We got her ready for bed on the first night and she happily went into her 'big bed' and watched us secure the cot-side. We had a wee black and white television in the caravan and Colin and I happily settled down with the luxury of a glass of wine to watch a film. Moments later we were shocked when the door of Lesley's wee room slid open and she stood confidently smiling at us. We had no idea how she could have got out of her bed with the cot-side in place and though we hadn't heard any sort of thud we hoped she hadn't got up over it. When we looked into the room it was to see that as usual, Lesley had managed to find a solution to being trapped when she didn't want to be – she had found loose spars in the frame and had simply removed enough to be able to squeeze through. We had to buy glue the next day to stop the intrepid explorer in her tracks. However, that wasn't before she had given us another laugh in the morning.

At home we had a fridge-freezer with the fridge section being at the top so Lesley had never had the opportunity for a raid on any goodies within. In the caravan the fridge was at floor level. We had left the door of our room slightly ajar so that we would hear her during the night and had been able to get her to stay in bed till early morning. As soon as it was light, she had managed her Houdini trick again and padded around the caravan holding on to anything that got her to the fridge. She then managed to sit down pulling the door open and the first thing she got her hands on was a tub of margarine – which she duly opened and began to devour in handfuls. That was our cue to get breakfast on the go for our hungry girl.

We had a great time in Whitley Bay enjoying walks along the front, the swimming pool and the fairground. I remember Colin and I being very hurt one night on a visit to the 'shows'. I had taken Lesley on to a children's roundabout ride and Colin had gone to pay. The first couple of times we went around, Colin was waving and smiling happily to us, sharing in Lesley's enjoyment. Then it was obvious that something had changed and he didn't look so happy. When we came off and I asked him what was wrong, he explained that the owner of the ride had taken his money but that when he had then noticed Lesley and the problems that she had, he had come back over and told Colin to take the money back as he wouldn't have charged if he had known that we had a child 'like that'. I have to say that the night was ruined for us at first as we felt denied normal family pleasure, but then we had to admit that the man was just being caring and trying to be kind. It was a learning moment for us that we needed to be careful not to over-react or take the wrong meaning out of well-meant gestures.

Back home, walking was still proving difficult for Lesley, partly because of her tiny, fused feet and partly because she had been left with no natural balance. Her legs were more than strong enough to carry her but she needed to have something to hold on to before she could make any progress. This was quite frustrating for her and she had a lot of falls during her attempts to make progress. However, the offer of a friend's no longer required baby walker with a base which held multi-coloured building bricks and completed by four wheels and a sturdy handle, was gratefully accepted and became Lesley's favourite toy. It was strong enough for outdoor as well as indoor use and gave our adventurous daughter the chance to get around with confidence – and seemed to raise her self-esteem. It was a joy for us to see her striding out under her own steam and obviously also built up her strength.

One day, in the height of summer 1980 when Lesley was around twenty months old, we were playing with her out in our front garden. We had been having a wee picnic sitting on a rug and I had got up and begun to tidy up. Lesley also then got to her feet and began to walk – but instead of the usual two steps and a fall, she simply continued till she reached Colin. We just couldn't believe our eyes – and cue Colin in tears! Doctors hadn't been able to give us much reassurance on whether there would be improvement in Lesley's ability to control the balance issues enough to walk unassisted and we had simply been trying to take things as they came. This was a huge day for us all and Lesley was so proud and delighted with our reactions to her success. These milestones that other people took for granted were like precious jewels to us and we so treasured them.

It was also around this time that we made a day trip one weekend to the House of the Binns which was quite near us. This is a historic house and seat of the Dalyell family and it is set in beautiful grounds. When we arrived we discovered that there was a guided tour about to start and we decided to sign up for it. We had a short time to wait so went back outside to have a look around and again Lesley gave us an emotional moment. Due to the formation of her upper and lower jaws, making the 'm' sound had been impossible for her and although she was saying Dad, Nana, Papa and various other words, she had not managed any attempt at Mum. Suddenly, while I was holding her in my arms, she looked at me, pursed her lips and in a loud clear voice said 'Mummmmmuummm' exaggerating the 'm' sound and then beaming with pride. I was thrilled of course and gave her lots of praise which she loved. She repeated it a number of times and got great reactions from us. However, it was then time for the guided tour of the mansion house and we went back inside to join the group. The lady leading the tour was quite formal in her approach and was not the least bit impressed to hear 'Mummmmmuummm' echoing repeatedly in the hallway. There was no option but for Colin to take Lesley out and leave me on my own to continue the tour – we could hardly ask our wee one to stop saying what we had waited a long time to hear!

Just after this milestone, Lesley had one of her routine check-ups at hospital and I mentioned that the turn in her eye seemed to be getting worse and showed up badly when she got tired. The doctor agreed and said that he would refer her to an optometrist for further investigations to determine the extent of the problem. Sometime went past and we got an appointment to go to Bathgate for eye tests. Obviously, at not yet two years old, Lesley couldn't just read the letters from a standard eye chart, but using a system of matching pictures and a child's eye chart, the lady explained what was required. I made sure Lesley understood and the test began. By the second test, Lesley had stopped responding and I thought she was bored or just not feeling like cooperating so I told her off. However, the optometrist was quick to tell me that she didn't think Lesley could see what was very clear to me and that we had reached the extent of her vision. I was totally shocked, never having thought that sight was such an issue for her. Various tests and visual examinations were carried out and a prescription for strong lensed spectacles was written up.

We were very fortunate to have a wonderful optician in Whitburn, Mr Wallace, and he went to huge efforts to have glasses made that fitted Lesley – the shape of her skull and the position of her ears and tiny button nose made this very difficult. I wondered how I was ever going to convince Lesley to wear them when she got them but I really needn't have worried. They must have opened up the world to her as she gladly wore them all the time. The only thing that annoyed her initially was if they slipped down her nose a wee bit so a piece of shirring elastic tied to each leg and anchored under the hair at the back of Lesley's neck easily solved this problem. We then had to 'patch' the lens of the good eye for a few hours a day to try to strengthen the weak eye, and this also worked and eventually solved the weakness without the need for surgery.

In the middle of all the major events of the first couple of years, some of the ordinary little checks were easily missed. When we attended Lesley's three-year old health visitor routine assessment it was discovered that her hearing had never been formally checked. There were no records to show that she could hear properly although I reassured the lady that she had always reacted well to noises and voices. However, the lady explained that she would need to test officially and record her findings so that this was in Lesley's notes.

She made a big thing of telling Lesley that they were going to play a game – which made my fun-loving daughter's eyes sparkle with anticipation. She explained that she was going to stand in one corner of the room while Lesley was to go and stand in the diagonally opposite corner. The health visitor was then going to whisper a word to Lesley, who was expected to say it back, thus showing that she could hear.

This obviously didn't seem like much of a game to Lesley but she did as she was asked and went to stand in her corner. The lady then crouched down, asked Lesley if she was ready and then, cupping her hands around her mouth, theatrically whispered 'CAT'. Lesley copied the crouching position, formed her own version of cupping her hands around her mouth, and equally theatrically whispered back 'DOG'!!! I couldn't help but laugh out loud and thankfully the health visitor had a sense of humour and quickly agreed that Lesley could certainly hear clearly – and was able to put adults in their place in a beautiful way.

We knew that in years to come there would be further operations required on Lesley's skull, mouth and face. Initially we had thought that there would also be work on her hands to give her separate fingers but this proved not to be an option. Lesley's hands were tiny and the worry was that surgery would leave her with stiff, weak digits which may not have any practical function and that she was better off with the strong grip she had using her thumb.

This gave us mixed emotions. There was relief that no more surgery was imminent but also disappointment that Lesley's hands couldn't be improved functionally for her. We already knew that there would be no surgery on her feet as the risks far outweighed any possible improvements but we had envisaged hand surgery. However, the greaseproof paper and blackcurrant cordial episodes had taught us that Lesley would find her own way to do things to the best of her ability, and we were happy to settle for hospital-free days for a while.

Croup continued to cause the biggest health issues in these early years but Lesley also had a terrible time when she contracted measles. She hadn't been able to have the usual vaccinations due to her underlying problems but had come through mumps and German measles with no cause for concern. However, one Christmas was dominated by the dreadful effects of measles for our wee girl. She was very ill and couldn't even keep sips of water down. She was prescribed anti-sickness medication but wasn't keeping that down either and she was delirious and trying to climb into Colin's aquarium. It took both of us to restrain her and keep her safe. She was eventually prescribed suppository form of the medication but this ended up causing an overdose which resulted in her speech becoming slurred and her face twisting to one side. It was terrifying to watch and we were scared that she had had a stroke. This was all made worse by the fact that it was the holiday period and the surgery was closed but we spoke to our wonderful pharmacist, Bobby Lumsden, who was able to tell us not to give her any more of the suppositories that night and to speak to the doctor in the morning. Within hours Lesley's face returned to normal and her speech was becoming clearer. We spent the night sponging her down to try to reduce her temperature and thankfully although it took some days for her to begin to properly improve, she didn't have another night like that one.

However, she again went through a dreadful time when she was three years old. It had been decided that if the epilepsy had indeed been caused by imbalance after all the big operations in her first year, things may have settled sufficiently for there no longer to be a problem. The fact that she had grown so much and not needed to have the medication increased tended to confirm this and I was asked if I wanted to try her off the two medicines. This seemed like a great idea and would be a big step forward if it worked so I agreed and was told to stop and monitor her condition carefully.

I happily – and innocently – did just that and our poor wee girl was left in the throes of withdrawal before our eyes. She was shaking and twitching and literally climbing the walls. She couldn't stay still and just didn't know what was wrong with her. Nothing we did helped her in any way and it was heart-breaking to watch. After a few hours of this we were pretty sure that it must be related to stopping the phenobarb and epilim so I gave her a small amount of each and after a wee while she began to settle. As soon as the surgery opened I phoned and asked to speak to a doctor for advice and was told I had not been given the correct procedure for stopping the medication. It was to take many weeks of cutting back a little each day of one medicine and then the same for the second until she was gradually off them both. If I had been told this at the beginning Lesley could have been spared a dreadful experience but as usual, she bounced back and didn't complain. It was Colin and me who were again left feeling utterly devastated by the things she had to bear. If she had been a whinging, sorry-for-herself type of child I think life would frequently have been hell but she just didn't dwell on bad times and as soon as she was feeling better, her wonderful smile was back in place and she was her happy, loving, adorable self.

It just worried me a great deal that she had to go through so much just to have a chance of a reasonable quality of life and we couldn't always spare her the pain and suffering. Perhaps all these early experiences were to shape her into the caring adult she was to become - someone who was very grateful for all the good times and didn't ever take people or things for granted.

Nursery School and Beyond

Our lives were able to become fairly normal and days, weeks and months went by with no major incidents to cope with. Lesley was making very good progress in lots of ways and I did a lot of work with her to introduce her to words and numbers and educational play. We had been offered a session with a home-school teacher who was able to regularly lend us a great variety of educational toys and games which really enriched Lesley's play and helped me to keep stimulating her and developing a range of skills. I also had a very detailed developmental milestones check-list which let me see areas of weakness so that I could focus on helping Lesley with aspects where her progress was slower.

I had registered Lesley for a nursery placement at the local primary school and at just over three years of age, in readiness for starting nursery in the August of 1982, we were asked to go for a visit to the school to meet the Infant Mistress. She told me that she wasn't sure that it would be right for Lesley to attend the school and I asked why. She talked about things like being toilet trained – which Lesley had been during the day long before she was two years old – and about coping with some of the physical things that would be expected of her. I explained that there was no problem with the toilet and that with all the child-sized furniture and equipment in the nursery, I couldn't see any problems.

I was then told that Lesley would need to be formally IQ tested to see if she would fit in to the mainstream school environment and that a visit to our home would be arranged by the educational psychologist before any position would be offered to us. This duly took place with me being asked to stay out of the way and out of Lesley's line of sight so that I could not give her any encouragement. When the report was sent in to the school it said that Lesley was inside the accepted IQ range and that she should be given her place. However, the Infant Mistress was still reluctant and suggested that Lesley should have a trial day so that the Nursery Teacher could monitor her more thoroughly. Again, this went very well and I was told that she had been a wee star and a pleasure to have in the nursery so we waited to hear that she would be enrolled. I then got a phone call from the Infant Mistress to say that Lesley could have one day a week at nursery and I told her that she already enjoyed that with the Mother and Toddler group and asked her why this was all that was on offer. She seemed surprised that I was not grateful for such a placement but I said that this would alienate Lesley from the other children who would quickly develop strong bonds with each other when they met up every day. She said that she thought Lesley might be quite strong-willed and this was the reason for her decision. I made myself stay calm and strong in spite of feeling extremely intimidated and more than a bit annoyed and said that I now understood – that all children who appeared to be strong-willed were simply given a one morning placement weekly and I asked how many children were in the same position as Lesley. She was very annoyed with me and said that we could have the full placement and see how it worked out.

It worked out very well and Lesley enjoyed her year at nursery and looked forward to going every day. In many ways it was probably one of the best years of her life. The other children quickly accepted her and at this point in her life she was a very friendly, confident and sociable child who thrived in the atmosphere and smiled her way through her year. I got to know the other mums who mostly all took to Lesley too – her smile and happy, friendly nature always won people over. It was here that I met my friend Lynne, mentioned earlier, and she and her family were to be lasting friends to all of us. Lynne and Frank had three children – Nicola who was a few years older than Lesley, Scott who was in Lesley's school class and Craig their youngest. Having fun with the three Paterson children who each had their very own natures was a great experience for Lesley who needed the opportunities of mixing with a family who didn't have an only child.

I remember the first time the whole family were to come for a visit with all of us. Colin and Frank had never met though Lynne had met Colin – but only if he arrived home early to head up to his home office to continue to work. She had thought he was quiet and reserved and had warned the children to behave and show respect. The only person who got into trouble that day was Colin who had all four children wound up and high as kites, hiding in cupboards and wardrobes at his instigation. It was priceless and Lesley had a ball – her usual fun with her Dad multiplied by three! The mixing and sharing and rough and tumble that siblings take for granted was missing for us and there were no better role models than the Paterson family for seeing the best of family life and for Lesley being able to be included in it.

I continued to work with Lesley at home too and she was making great progress with numbers, sounds and reading simple words. I was determined to give her the best start I could to help her to cope with school life and the difficulties that she would face. We bought a basic computer and I taught her to type so that if writing proved too difficult for her to keep up with, she would have the skills she needed. It was a little Sinclair Spectrum which was perhaps the start of her tie in with rainbows and all the bright colours of the spectrum! This was to be the beginning of Lesley's love affair with computers and in later years people were amazed by her skills and her typing - for someone with no fingers, she could outstrip most people with her speeds and knowledge and never failed to impress. When hand held computer games became popular, she was quickly 'hooked' on them too and her Uncle Kenny would often have to make himself work very hard to reach anywhere near the levels she got to on her games. She would sit casually, lolling in a chair, joining in the conversation as she played - and then announce scores that none of us could get close to.

Towards the end of the nursery year we were shocked to be told that Lesley would not automatically be given a place in Primary 1 and that she would need to be assessed again. This was upsetting as we felt that she had more than proved herself and the nursery staff gave her a good report. However, we jumped through the necessary hoops and Lesley was enrolled. The big day for starting school arrived and Colin managed to delay the start of his day to be at home to see her off. Dressed in her lovely purple blazer, with her hair in bunches with purple ribbons and carrying her school bag in her hand, Lesley made a beautiful picture and we were so proud – and of course, Colin cried again!

Lesley's Primary One teacher, Miss Cleland, gave her a lovely warm welcome and with a quick 'Bye Mum' over her shoulder, Lesley had started school. I walked home delighted that our wee girl had the confidence to embrace this new part of her life and the independence to be able to see me leaving with no tears and secure in the knowledge of my return. Schooldays weren't as relaxed or social as nursery had been but on the whole, Lesley enjoyed that first year and always held her teacher in high regard - in later years referring to her as 'my old teacher' to the disgust of Christine Cleland who was forever young! Colin and I were rather shocked by the poor standard of Lesley's colouring in when we attended parents' evening – the work was not as good as she could manage at home and I thought she was being lazy. However, her teacher explained that she had to use tiny, broken pieces of crayon and that she could only grip them under her hand, therefore she was unable to see what she was doing. I said that she had full-size crayons and coloured pencils in her bag but was told that the Infant Mistress said she had to use what everyone else used. This confirmed for us that she still disapproved of Lesley being there and couldn't see that we just wanted our daughter to have the chance to be socially accepted by the children who lived around her. Another learning moment for us but sadly the price was being paid by a five-year old child.

When her first school outing was planned for Edinburgh zoo, we were delighted as Lesley loved going to see the animals. By then I had managed to get a part-time job as a secretary so that I could leave after I saw Lesley to school in the morning and be home before her in the afternoon. I wouldn't have thought of offering to go on the school trip anyway as I wanted Lesley to have the experience of a day out with the other children rather than with her Mum. However, the Infant Mistress contacted me to say that the only way Lesley could go on the trip would be if I was going as well, so I agreed to go and arranged a day off. On the day, the children were divided into small groups – all except Lesley and a little boy who also had some mobility difficulties. They were both to be with me, on their own, and very much out of things. However, thankfully the other volunteer mums saw what was happening and said that as soon as we were told to head off, I should just join on with one of their groups so that my two wee charges didn't miss out on the group fun. I made sure that I wasn't 'available' for the next trip so that Lesley wouldn't be alienated from her friends and stuck with her mum and I was very grateful for the bonds that had been formed in the nursery environment that meant my daughter was accepted as 'one of the gang'.

Birthday parties in those days were always a huge success. We would have an afternoon party for all the children followed by an evening party for the adults in the family. This meant two cakes so I would always bake a cake in the shape of the appropriate number and a novelty cake to impress the children. These could be in the shape of Humpty Dumpty on the Wall, Crinoline Ladies, Gingerbread Houses, computers – anything that seemed relevant at the time and Lesley loved them. It was great for us to see her surrounded by her friends and just enjoying a thoroughly good time. Hallowe'en was also a great time in the early years. We wouldn't have had the money to have gone out and bought costumes but that didn't mean that Lesley went without the experience. She was everything from a Rubik's Cube to a White Rabbit, a Skeleton to a Domino and she just loved visiting our neighbours and her Nana and Papa and singing a song or saying a poem. Fun was paramount in these days.

It wasn't all plain sailing with older children in the school though. During the second half of Primary 1 Lesley began to have little 'accidents' at school and I couldn't get her to tell me why they were happening. It was strange that it was never a problem at home and indeed, Lesley had been very easily toilet trained as she hated being wet. Eventually we discovered, thanks to another child talking about it at home, that Lesley was being picked on by some of the older children. At break-times they were refusing to let her access the toilets and they were also walking around behind her mimicking her awkward walk. Lesley had to compensate for her poor balance by having a wide-legged gait and holding her arms out to the side and this was making her a target. I was told that even when she was walking home they were following her so I decided to try to see for myself before approaching the school.

Our house was near the school grounds and there was a path all the way with no roads to cross so Lesley had convinced me to allow her to make the trip on her own as she was very independent so I had to position myself where I could see her without being seen. Sure enough, at the end of the day, a group of boys were following her through the playground towards the gate to the path laughing and taunting as they walked like my wee girl. I hurried down towards them and told them that I would be reporting their behaviour – and that they should think shame of themselves to pick on a five-year old in such a way. We discussed it with Lesley that night and she admitted that it had been happening for a while and that it really upset her so we told her that she needed to let us know if people were treating her badly. Colin got home early the next afternoon and went to see if everything was all right as Lesley left the school grounds and was horrified to find that the boys were throwing stones at her as she walked up the path – though of course they ran off when they saw Colin.

I made an appointment to speak to the Infant Mistress – and to her credit she listened intently to what I had told her we had seen and been told about and she said that she was pretty sure she knew exactly who was at fault and that it would be dealt with immediately. She agreed that this would explain the toilet problems and was sorry that Lesley had suffered at the hands of the bullies. Thankfully, it did stop as did the wee accidents and I will always be grateful that what I had to say was taken on board and dealt with immediately.

We had a very worrying couple of weeks when Lesley was five years old. She very suddenly developed a stiff neck, high temperature and was in agony with pain in her head. I got an emergency appointment with our doctor and he thought it was either a shunt blockage or meningitis but couldn't be sure. He felt that the best thing would be for her to go straight into hospital and he phoned Sick Children's in Glasgow as he felt they could better liaise with the Southern General for background. They agreed that she should be brought in immediately and I managed to get in touch with Colin who came and picked us up. It was a scary journey in and Lesley was really suffering. On arrival we were quickly reassured that she was in good hands and very surprised when I was offered a folding bed in her room to be able to stay with her. This was such a relief and very different to her previous stays at the Southern General where parents were not allowed to stay. I can't describe how much easier it was to cope with it all when I could stay beside her and being in the hands of trained children's nurses was amazing. Colin still came every night after work but he could be more relaxed knowing I was with her day and night. I can remember developing a very sore throat and feeling scared that they would send me away. One of the doctors noticed that I had a problem – but instead of getting rid of me from the ward, she examined my throat, wrote a prescription for antibiotics and got me painkillers to ease the pain. My gratitude knew no bounds.

There followed days of tests which didn't get us any further forward as to what the problem was but after testing fluid tapped from the shunt, we were reassured that it wasn't meningitis and it didn't appear as though the shunt was blocked. Eventually Lesley began to improve and it was thought that one of two things had caused the problem. It may have been a viral attack or a delayed reaction to the typhoid injection she had the previous week.

She became quite a wee star in the second week of her stay as we were asked if we would be willing to take part in the doctors' final examinations which were taking part. I was not allowed to become involved other than to answer basic, general questions. Lesley was to answer anything she was capable of but the doctors had to make their own deductions from their examinations. Apert's syndrome was so rare that they were not expected to be able to come up with the name but they were expected to be able to identify all of the attributes from physical examinations and to do thorough medical checks as well.

In the beginning no one named the syndrome and some were better than others at identifying and naming correctly the symptoms. One young man kept asking Lesley 'has anyone else asked you about this' or 'has anyone else used one of these today' and he carried out his examination dependant on her responses which might not have been the best route to take. A young woman got very upset and ended up quite tearful. When the senior female doctor was speaking to me about her later she was quite scathing and said she might be better at home with her knitting. I was shocked and said that she was just very nervous – to which the doctor responded that if the young woman was the only one on duty the following week would I be happy to have my child's life in the hands of someone who just dissolved. A tough but understandable attitude and it was quite a lesson for me and I'm sure a much bigger one for the young doctor – I hope she made it.

By the second day, word had obviously got out and research had been done so some of the students knew the correct terminology. However, that made a few of them careless and they made assumptions like saying Lesley had a cleft palate after a cursory examination - which can be the case with Apert's – when she only had a very high palate. I thought another had made a mistake by observing that she had a heart murmur but when I commented on this later to the Professor I was shocked to find that she did indeed and that it was something that I had just never been told. Lesley coped well with these days and in fact it made the time pass very quickly in an interesting if still stressful way. A few years later she was invited to be a 'test case' again, this time at Bangour for the consultancy exams for plastic surgeons from all over Britain. Again she enjoyed her starring role and was the perfect patient – and it was a lot easier for me since she was healthy this time.

Good times outweighed bad times to the best of our abilities and probably our finest times as a family were when 'The Three Musketeers' went on holiday. In the early years, with little money behind us, these were usually caravan trips to places like Whitley Bay, Morecambe, Scarborough and Dornoch and we always had a ball. We would aim to have a lovely meal out at least once during our stay which was the highlight for Lesley and we just enjoyed relaxing in a caravan or chalet and enjoying seaside life – though Lesley was never a fan of playing in the sand. She hated the feel of it and didn't even want to walk on it as she couldn't cope with the 'movement'.

We stayed in an old fisherman's cottage in Scarborough when Lesley was three and a half years old. It was very quaint with only one little room on each floor and the toilet was right up in the eaves with access from a very narrow and twisting stairway which Lesley couldn't manage by herself. By the end of the holiday she had decided that she liked having company every time she needed to go to the toilet and refused to go on her own when we were back in our own house. She didn't get away with that for long but obviously thought it was worth trying.

Lesley had been given holiday money by her Nana and Papa and her Uncle Kenny as well as a wee bonus from us and she was excitedly planning what she might do with all of this money. I had always had a fear that it would be easy to turn Lesley into a spoiled little madam as being an only child with all the problems she had to cope with meant it would be easy to over-compensate materially. I therefore was careful to teach her values and make her save up for things she wanted. During the holiday she found a wonderful toy shop and had spent most of her money on the jigsaws she loved. As our final day approached, she realised that she still had money left and wanted to go back to the toy shop. I explained that she could always take some of the money home and spend it later but she was adamant that she wanted to buy something else. In the end, she bought for the sake of buying rather than because there was anything she really wanted.

When we came home I was going shopping and Kenny, who was off school, came with us. Lesley was thrilled and delighted to see that the supermarket had something she had been wanting for months – a £1.99 storybook and tape set of Pinocchio to add to her 'listen and follow' collection. I responded by saying that it was very sad that she had no money left and that she would have to save up before she could buy it. Kenny was shocked and offered to get it for her but I explained that I wanted her to value money and possessions and to be aware that she couldn't have everything even if it meant that the tape had gone before she could afford it. Thankfully it was still there a few weeks later and an important lesson had been learned. In actual fact, my daughter was the least materialistic person I have ever known and also the most grateful. With the difficulties she always had with numbers, her Dad and I agreed that she was the opposite of the people in life who knew the cost of everything and the value of nothing. Lesley knew the value of everything even if the cost was an unknown quantity to her and her thank you letters and phone calls or grateful hugs never failed to be an intrinsic part of her nature – so maybe the early lesson was important.

A week in a log cabin in Dornoch when Lesley was four was special because it was the first time we ever went out for dinner at night. We chose quite a 'posh' restaurant and wore our best clothes for the occasion. The owner of the cabins took a photograph of us and complimented us all on how smart we were looking and how grown-up our little lady appeared. Lesley was delighted. When we arrived in the restaurant we discovered that the other diners were all middle-aged or older and we immediately got the feeling that they were not best pleased to see a young child joining them in the room. However, Lesley's table manners were superb and her behaviour was excellent, so much so that we had people coming to us at the end of their meal to compliment her and to tell us how proud we should be of our wee girl. Needless to say, we were!

Not long after she had started school, Colin won an award from his company which was an all-expenses paid long weekend trip for two to Montreux on Lake Geneva. It just wasn't an option for us to go without Lesley. A two-night trip to London had been a previous award for Colin and we had left Lesley with my parents. However, it turned out that she had been in the first stages of whooping cough when we were away and it took away any pleasure in the trip. This time we made inquiries as to the possibility of paying to take her with us and in fact all we ended up having to do was pay for her flight.

Great excitement ensued with passports being applied for and arrangements made to go at the beginning of November not long before Lesley's fifth birthday. What an experience it turned out to be. Lesley was treated like royalty on the Swiss Air flight and to her delight she was invited to go to the cockpit with one of the stewardesses. On her return, with a beaming smile, she informed us that she had been up talking to 'the driver' which greatly amused everyone around. We were collected at the station by the head of the tourist agency in Montreux, a lovely man called Xavier. He took us to our hotel where a huge St Bernard dog was waiting to greet us at the top of the stairs on our arrival and Xavier arranged to take us out the next day to see the sights in the surrounding area. We went to the beautiful old village of Gruyere and visited the cheese factory, had a fondue in Chateau D'Oex and some apple strudel in Gstaad. The scenery was stunning and we felt like the rich and famous with our star treatment from Xavier. The following two days were free and we took the mountain railway to the top of Rochers-de-Naye where we walked in the bright sunshine with our jackets off, surrounded by deep snow. We toured Chateau Chillon, walked along the lake and generally just loved being tourists. The hotel life also appealed to Lesley and she loved getting her hot chocolate at breakfast time made with delicious Swiss chocolate – luxury.

This weekend left us all bitten by the travel bug and we made our minds up that we would save up to go abroad on holiday the following summer. We got a package deal to Spain and although the hotel was very basic, we had a great holiday. Lesley made friends with the Thomson holiday reps – they all adored her and made a great fuss of her every day. We bought tickets for their Gala night raffle and I was always left wondering if they fixed it when Lesley won the giant pink elephant that was one of the main prizes. She immediately called it Thomson in honour of her friends and he sat in a corner of her room.

An elderly couple moved in to the room next door to us at the start of our second week and they too quickly fell under Lesley's spell. She often chatted to them in the corridor or if we met them at dinner and she would tell them all about her day. After a few days, the lady hesitantly asked me if our wee boy was enjoying the holiday and I explained that we only had one child. She looked rather puzzled and said that she had heard us talking to him but hadn't ever seen him leave the room. She was obviously concerned and I didn't understand what she was meaning until she said that we always said hello to him when we entered the room and then goodbye to him as we left. The penny dropped because Lesley had been insisting that we always spoke to Thomson going in or out of the room so I had to take the lady to meet him and I think she was greatly relieved not to have a case of child neglect to report!

Lesley took to 'life abroad' though we had to resort to bribery to make her walk in the heat. Our hotel was half way between two little towns and there was nothing on our doorstep. This meant walking two or three miles in either direction if we wanted to see the sights and Lesley was not too enamoured. On the way there we would talk about getting a cold drink or an ice cream on arrival which usually worked well but returning was another story. By then she would be tired and her feet would be beginning to hurt – but she was a solid weight to carry. In came little, round Spanish lollipops which she loved – and we said that we couldn't carry her if she was eating a lollipop or we would be in a sticky mess. Thankfully for Colin and me she took this as fact and it would only usually be the last mile that required us to be carrying our five-year old back to the hotel which we were happy to go along with. Holidays with the Three Musketeers always meant a lot of laughs along the way even if things were difficult.

Having Fun and Special Moments

In Primary 2, girls in Whitburn have their first chance of being chosen to take part in the Gala Day, a major event on the West Lothian calendar and a great honour for those fortunate enough to be participants. On the day the names were being drawn out for the characters Lesley was off ill. Her wee friend ran along to tell us that Lesley's name had been pulled out and we were delighted to think that she was to be a Rainbow Fairy. Imagine our delight to find that she was to be the Rainbow Fairy Queen, one of the main roles and an amazing honour! There followed many Friday afternoons of her learning her role at rehearsals – she had to remove the crown from the retiring queen during the crowning ceremony after the parade through the town. Everything was precision planned and standards were very high so Lesley had to work very hard to master the formal curtsey as her balance problems made it difficult. We decorated the house and garden in the theme of 'Somewhere over the Rainbow' and we had around fifty guests coming after the formalities to share a buffet – and share our joy. Colin was working away from home at the time and just got back the night before but we had lots of help to get the decorations completed.

I have to say that this was by far the best day of my life! It was a little princess who walked downstairs that day in readiness for the big event and, as usual when these moments of great pride occurred, Colin shed a few tears! Lesley loved everything about it and smiled all day. She waved from the float to the people on both sides of the road who were calling out to her. She managed her important role well and loved having everyone back to her house afterwards. She wore a beautiful deep turquoise fairy dress with a sparkling tiara and later changed into a rainbow striped jumper I had made for her before going down to enjoy the fairground rides. It was a simply wonderful day and if she hadn't been accepted into the mainstream school setting, it is an experience we would all have been denied.

It was also the day that Kenny got engaged to Annie and this was the icing on the cake for all of us. Lesley and Annie had bonded very quickly so it was lovely for them to be sharing the special day. Two years later, also on Whitburn Gala Day, Kenny and Annie got married – and this gave Lesley the chance of another big day as they gave her the honour of being their wee flower girl. Her joy and excitement were infectious as she counted the days to the wedding. Lesley had a stunning full-length white dress with a pale peach sash at the waist. Once again she was a beautiful little princess and she played her part to perfection. She raised a smile for many of us during the ceremony when she used her order of service to gently waft Annie's veil rhythmically up and down from behind while the 'boring' bits were taking place around her. After the meal at the reception, when we asked where she was off to, she simply told us that she would be with the bridesmaids – obviously taking her role very seriously. She was like Annie's wee shadow and I think she would have followed her on honeymoon if we hadn't reined her in!

During her primary school days, Lesley was outgoing and up for anything. She loved to come home and go out on her bike on the paths around our wee estate. The bike had posed problems for us. Lesley desperately wanted to progress from her wee tricycle but we were concerned that balance would be a big issue and that working the hand brakes would be impossible for her because of her short arms and hand problems. However, my mantra was that she deserved to experience all that life had to offer her and even though Colin would have happily wrapped her up in cotton wool to protect her, he did agree that she hadn't gone through the big operations to then be treated like a prisoner in her own home. We visited a specialist bike shop in Glasgow and outlined our concerns. They said that there were plenty of suitable bikes with stabilisers that could be removed if that proved to be an option in the future and they offered to come up with back-pedalling brakes that would mean Lesley didn't need to rely on her hands. Positioning of the handles and seat could be adjusted to give her the optimum chance of coping and gaining success. With all of this taken care of she could concentrate on gripping the handlebars without having to take her hands off to reach and pull on the brakes.

We were most grateful and a bike was chosen, the adaptations made and very soon Lesley was whizzing around confidently under her own steam. Losing the stabilisers didn't take long either and we were thrilled with the delight on Lesley's face as she got around under her own steam. You may be wondering how successful the back-pedalling brakes proved to be and I would have to say that they were scarcely ever used – not because Lesley went so slowly that she didn't need them, but because she discovered that a bit of a pull on the hand brakes coupled with dropping her legs down behind the pedals was the best way to stop the bike! I can't count the number of times I was asked about the black bruises all the way up each of her shins and I know there were strangers who must have thought she was suffering at someone's hands. However, Lesley would quickly explain to anyone who commented that it was the best way to stop her bike and we didn't ever bother having adaptations made for her later bicycles.

Socialising and mixing continued to be something that I knew to be very important for Lesley. She got this at school and at Sunday school but I wondered if one of the local Brownie packs would be willing to give her a place so that she could develop skills in a less formal setting. My friend Lynne's daughter had attended the Friday night Brownies so she was able to give me the Brown Owl's name and I duly went down to meet her when Lesley turned seven years old. I was a wee bit nervous of rejection considering the nursery and school experience and could hear myself 'rabbiting on' a wee bit about hoping she could have a chance to see how she would get on at Brownies in spite of her problems. Mrs Russell had no qualms whatsoever and was genuinely surprised that I was asking with such concern. As far as she was concerned, Lesley was the right age, lived in Whitburn and there was a vacancy – so she could start the next week. We were delighted that this was something else she could experience and it proved to be one of the best things we ever did. It turned out to be Barbara, Mrs Russell's assistant in the unit, who worked most with Lesley and Lesley simply adored her.

Her Brownie membership gave her the opportunity to go away to camp for a weekend, something that I was a bit wary of – mainly because though I loved caravan holidays I had no fondness for the thought of camping in a tent. Lesley was desperate to go and it was with great excitement that she left after school on the Friday to head west for the weekend. What a weekend of rain it turned out to be. I lay in bed early on the Saturday morning listening to the rain hammering on the window and worrying about how Lesley would be coping with such conditions for her first camping experience. The rain didn't really abate by the time they were due home late afternoon on the Sunday and we went to collect her fearing the worst. Our daring daughter was last off the bus, blethering to Mrs Russell and looking rather dishevelled and, frankly, grubby! However, what a smile we were given when she noticed us waiting with our hearts in our mouths and she immediately shouted that it had been brilliant and she hadn't wanted to come home so soon! This was an aspect of her nature that she didn't get from me as neither the camping nor the weather would have left me smiling. Her next camp was in much better weather – but the field they had been allocated had been absolutely full of nettles, though needless to say, Lesley had no complaints at all.

She did very well during her Brownie years and later moved on to Guides and Ranger Guides where Martha, Biff and Pamela were to become her mentors and friends. Camping, working for badges and taking part in parades were some of the experiences on offer and Lesley did so well that she ended up being presented with the Baden Powell award in recognition of her successes in Guiding – all thanks to Mrs Russell for welcoming her into the movement in the first place.

Further holidays during these early primary school years also allowed Lesley to meet other people and she was often able to make friends with children staying in the same hotels as us. We met a lovely family when we stayed in Belgium and their daughter and Lesley hit it off enough for us to have a couple of excursions together. Likewise, in Italy she met a lovely girl whose own little brother had some difficulties and which probably helped her to be so friendly towards Lesley. I remember the four of us going to a fun-fair one night and having a great time till a thunderstorm rolled in very suddenly and we had to run all the way back to the hotel. Lesley thought it was hilarious that we all arrived back drenched in our summer clothes.

On that same holiday in Lido Di Jesolo, we went out for a walk one night and we decided to have a coffee in a café on the long promenade. We sat outside on a raised decked area at the front corner of the café and there was a lane running alongside below us. Lesley noticed that there were two little boys around her own age playing football in the lane and she got up on her knees on her chair to lean on the railing to watch them. The boys noticed her and after a quick chat with each other they waved Lesley down to join them. Her face lit up as she asked if it was all right for her to go and we gladly gave permission. We had a most relaxing hour while the happy threesome had a great time together with no need to worry about verbal communication. Football transcends language, cultures and nationalities and the family oriented Italian people embraced our little daughter as just being a lovely child and her disabilities made no difference to her simply being a child to make a fuss of. In these early years our confident, warm and friendly wee girl drew friends to her and it was a joy to see.

The only other operations in the primary school days were relatively minor though anaesthetics were always worrying. Lesley had a few oral surgery procedures in Canniesburn hospital due to her having extra rows of teeth erupting in her upper palate and also because some of the teeth that were meant to be there were coming in at right angles. Lesley coped with these operations remarkably well and her positive attitude was commended. One doctor brought her a single rose after one of the operations in recognition of her bravery and her wonderful smile – and she positively glowed in his praise. On the morning after another operation when she had lots of stitches in her mouth, I was appalled when I arrived to find her having a roll for her breakfast. I thought the nurses must be cruel to expect her to bite and chew this rather chunky item and my face must have registered my concern. One of the nurses was quick to tell me that Lesley had already finished the soggy cereal they had thought might be best for her to tackle – and it was my hungry daughter who had asked if she could have one of the rolls she had seen other people eating. The nurses couldn't believe it, but with Lesley's appetite always being very healthy, I wasn't surprised – and of course she finished the roll!

With no major operations to worry about, Lesley had a chance to lead as normal a life as possible. In those days, anything that was unusual in her development was simply put down to being part of the Apert's Syndrome umbrella and autism was never considered.

However, on looking back it is apparent that there were early signs of the condition that was to prove difficult for her to handle later. Lesley would have obsessions, some more difficult to deal with than others, and she also liked everything to be very well-planned and organised and hated last minute changes. As soon as she could write she loved to make lists and watching Coronation Street, her favourite television programme, was an intense experience for her. As characters appeared on the screen during the programme she would write their names down. Then at the end of the programme when the titles rolled, she would tick off the names one by one. If she was left with one that hadn't been ticked on her list she got really upset and Colin and I learned that the best thing to do was to say that we had seen the name and she must just have missed it on screen. That way she could tick it off and be happy – she couldn't cope with having a name on her list that she didn't think had been credited.

Another obsession that caused considerable annoyance for me around this time was picking off the wallpaper in her room. Looking back, it is very easy to understand why she did it, but at the time it just seemed like naughtiness. Lesley had a high cabin-style bed with drawers and cupboards underneath. We would take her to bed, read her a story and get her settled down but as soon as she was left on her own, she began to pick off the wood-chip wallpaper. She would get a row for doing it, get upset about being told off and promise never to do it again – only to continue the next night. If I had known about autism at that time I would probably have realised that Lesley hated the feel of the rough wood-chip paper and we could have saved ourselves a lot of trouble by simply re-doing the wallpaper in her room. However, hind-sight is a wonderful thing and we just have to accept that we didn't understand the issue enough to make it better for Lesley at that time.

Some aspects of her early home-life gave Lesley a lot more pleasure than the wood-chip wallpaper. Another part of her desire for routine came in the form of liking to have home-made soup for lunch every day followed by a slice of my fruit loaf so baking and soup making were regular occurrences. When she had her morning place in nursery I went down to collect her and we came home and enjoyed our soup together. The kitchen in our house had been of very poor quality and we decided to update it and took the opportunity to fit in a breakfast bar which was ideal for the three of us and would be in a previously unusable recessed area. On the day after the kitchen had been completed I had none of my own soup left and with all the clearing up, there was no time to make any. I searched in the cupboard and found a packet mix of soup which I hastily made up in a large pot and hurried off to collect Lesley. She was extremely excited at the thought of having lunch at the new breakfast bar perched on top of the high bar-stool which really appealed to her. I dished up the soup, saying nothing about it, but my daughter's highly honed taste buds were not to be fooled. She took one spoonful of soup, paused, placed the spoon back in the bowl and asked me what kind of soup I called it. I replied that it was vegetable soup and she very disdainfully informed me that there must be something wrong with the vegetables because it wasn't good soup. She had very good taste – but I have to say that the rest of that lunchtime conversation showed that tact was not her strongest point.

We had switched on the fluorescent lighting which had been installed under the units above the breakfast bar and they were very effective. When Lesley had reluctantly finished the disappointing soup, she rested her head on one hand and gazed lovingly at me in the glow of the new light. I asked her what she was thinking and she replied that I really reminded her of someone – Bruce Forsyth. Now at that time she adored Bruce Forsyth when he was on the game show that she enjoyed and I asked her if it was his smile or his joking that I was reminding her of. Unfortunately, she responded promptly that she had just noticed that I had the same wrinkles on my face that Bruce had – at least twenty-five years my senior! I decided that use of the new lights might be an over-rated luxury that I could manage without.

Eating the soup reminds me that fine motor control was difficult for Lesley but she usually just kept developing her own ways to cope with manual tasks. One of the most difficult things for her was eating with a spoon – and in the very early days of eating things like soup or yogurt on her own, more was spilled than made it into her mouth. Step up her Papa who could see what the problem was and spent a day in his garden hut with some spoons from the house, bending the handles until he had come up with a design that worked. Lesley was thrilled to be able to eat on her own without losing the contents of her spoon and her Papa kept one of his designs at their house, giving us the others to take with us. We carried one everywhere in those early years so that she was never at a disadvantage again. The manufacturers of Tommee Tippee products for babies should have signed my Dad up and they would have made their fortune earlier! Lesley's determination and love of food combined to help her to develop the cutlery skills she needed and once her hands had grown a wee bit and her thumbs had more movement, she managed just fine with any design provided.

I did learn quickly that there was no point in trying to talk Lesley into agreeing to a particular piece of clothing that I thought was lovely but that she didn't like. If it was the feel of the material or the way an item felt when it was on, she just wouldn't ever wear it and the first thing Lesley would do on being shown a possible new item of clothing would be to feel the material. If that didn't meet with her approval there was no point in even trying the item on. Some brand new outfits were donated to charity shops because I got it wrong at the beginning. Her dislike of loud noises like fireworks, and bright lights or the glare of sunlight was also easily explained after we learned about the sensory issues of autism. Lesley didn't go anywhere without her prescription sunglasses as she couldn't tolerate bright sunshine, even on winter days. We don't beat ourselves up with regrets over things we didn't fully understand in those days because we know we always loved her and did what we thought was best to help our special daughter – and that's all anyone can ever do.

Doing what was best wasn't always easy. Lesley came in from school one day when she was in an upper primary class at school and gave me a letter. It contained information about a proposed trip to Beecraigs Country Park for a day of outdoor education and it outlined the things on offer and asked if we wanted a place for Lesley. Reading about kayak canoeing, mountain biking and abseiling made my heart sink. I couldn't see any way that she could possibly cope with such things but I hated having to tell her that she would need to miss out particularly as she was very keen to go. Reluctantly, after talking to Colin about it at night, I ticked the 'no thank you' box and signed the form, explaining our decision to Lesley.

Imagine my surprise a few days later when I received a phone call from the outdoor education officer for Beecraigs asking why I wasn't giving my permission. I began to explain that although I would have loved her to attend my daughter had various physical problems that would preclude her from taking part. The gentleman amazed me by saying that he had already met Lesley on a visit to the school and had assessed the issues – and he was more than happy to find ways of letting her take part! I don't know who was more thrilled, Lesley or me though Colin took a bit more convincing as he was still very protective of her. She would have someone doing the abseiling in tandem with her in case she hit problems, the mountain bike course wouldn't be more than she could handle and her hands could be strapped to the canoe paddle so that she didn't have to try to hold on to it, just control it.

The day arrived. We had been given information about suitable clothing and about packing a complete change of clothes in case it was needed and Lesley went off with great excitement and anticipation. Lynne and I had an afternoon each week where we met up at each other's house and the children knew to come there at the end of the school day and that day it was my turn to be at Lynne's home. Her son Scott was in Lesley's class and also going on the trip and we watched for them coming home with a degree of nervousness over how the day would have gone. As soon as I saw Lesley approaching, I knew that she was wearing the alternative clothes – and her hair was plastered to her head. She had obviously been in the canal! Anxiously I waited for her to come in but was immediately reassured by her beaming smile and reports of the day having been brilliant. Scott and Lesley reported on all that had happened with great enthusiasm and positivity with no mention of the need for Lesley's change of clothes so I had to ask if there had been any problems. They replied that no, everything had been great and then very casually, Lesley said that, by the way, she had fallen in the canal – but only after she had completed her canoeing and simply because she hadn't waited for someone to help her to get out. Obviously it didn't even register with her that this could have been a real problem and it in no way wasted her enjoyment of the day.

She deserved much admiration for her positivity but school wasn't always easy with some teachers more able to accept her than others. Her reading and spelling progressed very well, in fact her spelling was simply superb and her reading was fluent even if her comprehension didn't always match up in later years. However, number work was another matter altogether and this caused many tears in our home – not always just Lesley's! In Primary 2 she was introduced to the Cuisenaire Rods system for counting and just couldn't cope. These are different sized coloured pieces of wood with a long one representing the number ten and decreasing in size down to a tiny cube to stand for number one. For addition and subtraction, it was necessary to balance individual rods on top of the ten-sized rod and do the necessary calculations. With the hand problems she had, Lesley just couldn't manage without knocking some off and coming up with the wrong answer. In the house I had shown her how to use a simple number strip to do basic arithmetic and this worked very well. One night she was playing an addition game on her computer with a friend from her class and getting the answers correct first every time. Her wee friend stated that it was a shame she couldn't use the number strip in class because then the teacher wouldn't be shouting at her all the time! Out of the mouths of babes indeed! I asked to see the teacher to discuss this but was told that all of the children had to use the rod system and Lesley would just have to work harder to cope. As a caring teacher myself I just couldn't get my head around these attitudes. I knew that having Lesley in the class meant that additional thought had to go into normal situations but she was a lovely, friendly, helpful wee girl who was loved by those who got to know her and it was sad when occasionally she suffered at the hands of those who should have known better.

The first months of Primary 3 were much better and she was making great progress and growing in confidence but sadly Miss Dunleavy left half way through to go into the ministry and the church's gain was teaching's loss. One primary school year made us feel we had reached the end of the road with mainstream education. A meeting with the head teacher to explore our options 'reassured' us that Lesley wasn't the only child struggling to cope with the teacher's methods and that she was still actually doing quite well and the following year was completely different because the teacher used praise and positive reinforcement instead of criticism and negative comments and Lesley flourished.

An incident during the year with a teacher who just couldn't take to Lesley, brought a day which shames me still. I arrived to collect Lesley for a hospital appointment and the teacher came to the door and furiously told me that my daughter had lines and a letter of apology to write to another child because she had stabbed him with a pencil. I was shocked as this was most unlike Lesley and I was very angry with her for doing such a thing. The whole way to Bangour Hospital had me haranguing her for her dreadful behaviour, going on and on about how wrong it was and how the lead in a pencil could cause harm. Lesley sat in the back seat saying nothing.

When we arrived at the hospital, the nurse told a very subdued Lesley to undress down to her underwear and when she took her tights off, I almost fainted. The whole thigh area of both legs was covered in gouged pencil marks and large livid weals. Lesley then had the chance to tell me what had actually happened at school that day. The boy had been continually stabbing her under the desk with his pencil and she had tried telling the teacher three times but was simply sent back to her seat. Finally, in desperation, she jabbed him once on his hand – and of course he went straight to the teacher and showed her the mark, with Lesley then being the butt of the teacher's fury and completely unable to tell her side of the story to someone who wouldn't listen.

The incident highlighted just how little respect this teacher had for my child, but the most upsetting part of the story was my part in it. I had to apologise to my wee girl for letting her down by my instant reaction and she just clung to me and cried in the hospital changing room. I felt like the worst parent there had ever been. When we got back home, I told Lesley that it was still wrong for her to have retaliated in the way she did and she agreed. Her letter of apology however was dictated by me – and it said that she was sorry for stabbing the boy once with her pencil even though he had been stabbing her all day on both legs with his. I gave Lesley a letter from me to give to the teacher in which I told her that if the children happened to be having a P.E. lesson that day and Lesley took her tights off, she would see that both legs were still in a dreadful mess with weals, bruises and lead marks. I said that I was ashamed of myself for not allowing Lesley to explain the incident and that I should not have taken the teacher's version as fact when I knew this was not my child's normal behaviour. I also said that she had apologised for her retaliation but that she would not be doing the lines since she was much more sinned against than sinning. The head teacher phoned me at my work that day to say that I was never to give Lesley a letter to give to her teacher again as this could make Lesley feel that I was undermining her teacher. In future if such incidents occurred, I was to post the letter! Lesley, of course, got no apology – other than from me.

The rest of that year remained one of the worst for us as a family as Lesley had much criticism to cope with and no praise. Her end of year report gave all the negatives and not a single positive – things like saying her handwriting was untidy, but not qualifying it by saying that considering her hand problems, it was miraculous that it was legible at all. I did speak to the head teacher again and he apologised for signing it without asking for other comments to be added. He said that off the top of his head he would have said that Lesley was cheerful, helpful, friendly, caring and hard-working – but none of these comments went down on paper and my wee girl was left with a report that simply highlighted the aspects of her life that were difficult anyway without acknowledging the huge efforts she was making to cope and fit in. It was little comfort to speak to other parents at the end of that year who said that they were so relieved the end of term had come because they had endured the worst school year possible for them and their child. Sad, and no credit to a professional who should have been looking at the whole child, not just the bits she considered to be negatives.

I mention these incidents in passing to give more detail of Lesley's story. It is worth mentioning that sometimes teachers forget the impact they have on a child's life and that of the family at home who have to try to pick up the pieces if things go wrong. The child with additional needs in a class did not ask to be there and would not have chosen to have the problems life has given them and it is the role of the good teacher to try to accommodate the child, meet the needs and play a part in helping the child to achieve whatever their best can be. Colin and I had many very unhappy times caused by the worries of school life and I regret some of the hours I spent making Lesley go over and over things which she simply wasn't capable of learning in relation to number work. Her abilities in reading and spelling and using a computer should have been celebrated rather than her heart being broken over her weakness with arithmetic.

On the day of her final sport's day at primary school, I finished work early enough in the afternoon to get up to the school to watch the fun. The Infant Mistress saw me standing at the top of the banking watching the action and I was quite surprised when she chose to come over to stand with me. As the children took part on the grass below us, she said that it almost didn't seem possible that Lesley was ready to move on to secondary school and I agreed that the years had flown by. Her next words were most unexpected though a great delight to me. 'She's done rather well,' she said and I proudly agreed!

Secondary School and Social Difficulties

Moving on to secondary education was a big step for Lesley. At this time, I had been working in the library of Whitburn Academy for a few years and knew the set up well. I was concerned about Lesley's acceptance in the large setting where she would meet hundreds of people who didn't know her and who would perhaps introduce her to a level of rejection that she hadn't previously been aware of. I also wondered about the reactions of the staff, particularly in departments like science and technical studies where Lesley's physical difficulties could cause additional problems.

In the first year she was something of a 'novelty' for the other children in her class and many of the girls from Fauldhouse and Longridge who had not known her before made quite a fuss of her and tended to 'mother' her. She also seemed to get on well with most of her teachers though of course there were some who showed some reluctance. Recently Colin and I met two of the teachers who knew her in those days, one of whom taught her P.E. and was her Guidance Teacher for some years. The other teacher told us that not only had Lesley been a joy to have in the school – his words – but that in those days when teachers were more inclined to feel like saying 'no' when asked about having a child such as Lesley in the mainstream environment, Lesley taught people to say 'yes'. That is a wonderful accolade and makes us feel that Lesley probably made it easier for other children in later years to be given a fair chance without ignorant prejudice clouding their acceptance – quite a legacy. For Lesley, although walking around the school was tiring, the act of moving on to different classes with different teachers every hour was a good thing and she enjoyed the variety.

Sadly, the early peer acceptance and levels of inclusion tailed off by the end of that first year and Lesley became more and more isolated in her second year. Other factors conspired to make this a difficult period for her and life became very trying. With puberty kicking in at the same time that her peers were leaving her out of things, Lesley became much less confident in herself and began to be more attention seeking. She latched on to adults in the school who she felt liked her but she couldn't tell where to draw the line with them. She resorted to phoning Childline at lunchtimes from the pay phone to give her someone to speak to when she was left on her own. I ran a board games club in the library during lunch breaks for children like Lesley who needed somewhere to belong and she joined it and another lunch club that gave her access to computers but that still left her very isolated – and lonely - at other times. The more vulnerable she felt, the more attention seeking she became and I had to work very hard with her to try to get her to understand that she could make people turn against her if she was too demanding. The obsessive tendencies - which we would later understand to be part of her autism – were also becoming more apparent and a bigger issue than previously.

Puberty was not being kind to our daughter and many of the issues upset her a lot and she struggled to cope. Bad acne, particularly on her body coupled with having to cope with periods and wearing a bra were things she hated. She also had to put up with some bullying by a small group of boys in her class led by one in particular. They would do silly, infantile things like hide her pencil case or her school bag so that she couldn't find what she needed in a class. Lesley always wore her bag on her back when she was walking in the corridors so that she had her hands free to improve her balance. This allowed the boys to wait for her at swing-doors and then trap her in the doors with her on one side and her bag on the other. I pleaded with her to let me take it further but she got very upset and said that it would just make them pick on her more. I was later to regret not doing what I knew to be the right thing.

As if this wasn't enough for her to be coming to terms with, a major change in our lives happened in the May of 1991 when I was diagnosed with breast cancer which was terrifying for all of us. My only concern was that I simply had to make it out the other side no matter what it took because Lesley needed me so much – and this was what I told my surgeon and oncologist. For a while the news kept getting worse – the initial lumpectomy showed that there was spread and that a mastectomy was needed. Then it was discovered that there was spread to the chest wall and lymph nodes and things looked worse. We worked hard at keeping everything as normal and calm as possible for Lesley but it wasn't easy and we worried about her ability to cope.

Thankfully I had an excellent surgeon who promised that he would do everything in his power to remove all traces and as a back-up arranged five weeks of radiotherapy. I was otherwise fit and healthy so the surgery, although traumatic, did not make me feel ill and I decided to sign myself off and go back to work even before the radiotherapy started. I felt that this would give Lesley the message that all was well – and be good for my own morale too. Problems with fluid build-up meant that initially I had to return to hospital to be aspirated most afternoons but the surgeon assured me that this was a very good sign. The fact that he was sure that he had removed all the lymph nodes meant that initially the fluid had nowhere to go so I had to be very grateful to him.

By the time the radiotherapy was due to start it was almost school holiday time so Lesley came to Edinburgh with me every day and we tried to turn the trips into days out. The café at the Botanic Gardens near the hospital became one of our favourite spots and we also went berry-picking on the way home a couple of times. On two occasions Colin was working in Edinburgh and we met up with him for lunch and one day he took time off in the afternoon so that he could take Lesley with him after lunch. They climbed Arthur's Seat, the volcanic hill near Edinburgh city centre which gives a good view of Easter Road Stadium where Hibs play. Keeping things as light and normal as possible helped us all to cope and made it easier for Lesley to feel all was well.

We had to cancel our summer holiday that year which was a real negative for my travel loving daughter but we managed to fit in a week to Morocco during the October holiday week. Lesley still loved to get away for holidays or weekends and we loved to do things which gave her a buzz. As a huge Coronation Street fan, it was a real treat to take her to the Granada Studios for the full tour and she loved it. 'Emmerdale' country and James Heriot's 'All Creatures Great and Small' setting also went down well since these were programmes she enjoyed.

By this stage in Lesley's life a difficult scenario was beginning to emerge. When she wasn't coping well with relationships or having problems with school work, she learned to put on a front – but the backlash took place at home. Her violent mood swings became very difficult to deal with and although it didn't happen often, the rages which took over had all of us wrung out at times. We hadn't thought of autism then and anything that was difficult to cope with came under the 'Apert's umbrella'. Looking back, we could possibly have helped her more but all we could do was try to talk her through her problems and give her our reassurance and love. She was still the most loving and caring person but one who found life beyond coping with at times. People would talk about her in glowing terms, saying that she always had a beautiful smile and that 'you always got her in the same happy mood'. If only, but it was reassuring to know that Lesley kept her pain and anxieties reined in until she was safe in her own house and no one else ever took the brunt of the rages. However, it was all having a really bad effect on her self-esteem and her confidence was being eroded. The happy-go-lucky and up-for-anything wee girl was disappearing and short of a magic wand, we were unable to give her an easier life experience.

Probably the hardest times were when Lesley had treated me very badly for hours and sometimes days on end but would then be utterly distraught when she had calmed down and realised all that she had said and done to the mum she adored. She would be almost inconsolable and always promised that it would never happen again, though of course it did. I will always be grateful for the strength of our family bond as without it I don't think we would have remained intact. In fact, the bond was probably closer because of the difficulties rather than in spite of them but it wasn't something that was easy to achieve and Colin and I had to really concentrate on the positives which was often very draining. Unless you have lived through it, it is very difficult to comprehend the stresses put on the whole family when the autistic child – or adult - is not coping. It is easy to assume that parents must be exaggerating if the bad behaviours are not displayed outside the home and many professional people have a real ignorance of how bad things can be. Emotions are pushed to the limits and it is only love and patience that gets you through and focussing on the good times is vital.

When Colin's football team, Hibs, won the League Cup in 1991 just after we returned from Morocco, Lesley was so tuned in to his excitement that she said she would like to start going to Easter Road with him to support Hibs. This was much to my disgust as a Rangers fan but Lesley had sussed that she couldn't rely on me taking her to Ibrox Stadium in the same way as she could depend on her Dad taking her to watch Hibernian! Colin agreed but I really wasn't sure that she would enjoy the experience with noise and crowds not being her favourite things to deal with. For her first match I told her to take one of her hand-held computer games with her so that she had something to focus on if she got bored. I nagged her about not wasting the game for her Dad by asking how much longer it would last or wanting to leave early and told her just to try to put up with it if she wasn't enjoying herself. I needn't have worried. She was hooked from that first match and became a passionate Hibs supporter and no Dad could have had a son who shared the love of the sport as much as she did. Even getting hit full on the face by the ball during that first game didn't put her off. In fact, it probably added to her enjoyment because one of the officials was sent to make sure she was all right and to treat her to a drink and biscuits which greatly impressed her and made her feel part of things. This was the start of a wonderful football bond between Lesley and Colin and the knowledge she developed and her retention of facts and names meant they could have some great discussions about the sport in general. Supporting Hibs wasn't always easy if results were poor but the shared experiences and love of the club they both had never wavered. They became season ticket holders and for many years attended all home games as well as many away games.

With her growing love of all things related to Hibs, Colin decided to invite my Dad to go with them for a stadium tour of Easter Road on a non-match day. My Mum and I went into Edinburgh with them but had a wander around the shops of Princes Street while they went down to Leith. We had arranged where we would meet up again afterwards and it was obvious when we were reunited that they had all had a really good time. Lesley told us about all that they had seen and done and was thrilled to have been into the dressing rooms and the board room and to have her hands on a recently won youth trophy. My Dad embarrassed her greatly by repeating what she said when he asked if she had enjoyed it. 'Absolutely,' she had replied, 'it was better than sitting in the house doing nothing.' That became a standing joke in the family for all worthwhile experiences from that day onwards. Lesley was to go on to enjoy many more stadium tours in the future with Colin when they were treated to corporate match-day tickets for birthday or Christmas presents but that first experience was one of the best.

Occasionally we would have one of Lesley's flare-ups happening on a Saturday just before it was time to leave to go to a match and she would simply refuse to go. No amount of cajoling got through to her and it would end up with Colin not going either. A black mood would descend in the house for the rest of the day – particularly if it turned out to have been a good win for the team. However eventually we discovered that Lesley hated the heightened atmosphere of the big Hearts, Rangers and Celtic games and she was able to tell us that she would prefer never to go to them. These had obviously been the days when her mood would have caused problems but she simply hadn't been able to vocalise her feelings. Again, if only we had been tuned in to the autism earlier we may have recognised that there was a pattern emerging, but once we were aware, there was never another match that she avoided and Colin also enjoyed choosing the games they attended instead of having season tickets and going to all matches.

The passion she had for the game included an obsession with collecting autographs and she gathered hundreds over the years. Colin had the patience of a saint when it came to helping her to get them. Shouting to players during warm-ups before the games didn't always work and it really frustrated Lesley if they ignored her. So Colin would take her in to Edinburgh hours early so that she could wait for players arriving and allow her to grab her chance of meeting up with those she needed to sign her book. It was often the new signatures that gave her most pleasure regardless of the final score of the match. She had created a spreadsheet and took great delight in typing up her new additions as soon as she arrived home. The collection would go on to include Speedway stars and any celebrities she met and her autographs books were her most precious, priceless possessions.

Making the Best of Life

Bad times were greatly outweighed by good times and we tried to get as much out of life as we could. I had always had a strong drive to save as much money as possible to provide for Lesley's future and although we now had more disposable income, we had always saved rather than spent more. After my brush with cancer, I realised that it was more important to focus on shared good times when we were all together, just in case she was going to lose her Mum early. My prognosis had not been wonderful after the surgery and it put things into a different perspective for us all. Since our greatest love as a family was travelling, we decided to aim for better holidays and to begin to see and experience more of the world and its peoples and cultures.

Lesley was still enjoying her membership of the Guides but with her school friendships lessening we wanted her to have another interest. After a lot of thought, she had decided that she would like to try horse-riding and we approached a local riding stables to see if they thought she would cope. They were happy for her to try it and Lesley really enjoyed the experience and took to it confidently so this gave her something else to focus on and keep her busy and involved. Her Aunt Nette, who had her own horse and loved riding, was able to advise us about where to go for a riding hat and to find boots that would go on Lesley's feet and she was delighted that Lesley was enjoying the experience of riding.

There were less hospital appointments to fit in at this stage and I decided that the time was right for me to return to teaching. After I had recovered from the radiotherapy I applied to do an evening refresher course at Moray House College in Edinburgh in preparation for going back to my career. Everything went according to plan and in February 1992 I finished at Whitburn Academy and was on the supply teaching list. Some of my colleagues wanted to take me out for lunch on my last day and the library was closed to allow this to happen. A former librarian had been invited to come back from Fife for the occasion and the two of us stayed for an extra coffee when the others returned to school.

I then went back down to Whitburn Main Street to wait for Lesley coming out and to give her a lift home. A group of pupils ran towards me when they saw me in the car and said that Lesley had fallen down the stairs and that I needed to go down to the main entrance. When I arrived, it was to discover that Lesley hadn't simply fallen; she had been pushed down the marble staircase by one of the boys who had been picking on her. The fact that her bag was on her back had probably saved her from cracking her head on the stairs but she was obviously in a great deal of pain. She said that her leg really hurt but that she needed the toilet and would I help her to get there. The teacher who was with her told me just to use the staff toilet nearby and Lesley hobbled there, as usual being very brave when life was proving tough.

All she wanted was to get home so I managed to get her out to the car and then into the house. We were thinking that she might have pulled a muscle in the fall so I asked her if she wanted to have a soak in a warm bath and this appealed. I got her upstairs and into the bath and when she came out we made her comfortable on the couch and she seemed to be in less pain. When Colin came home and she tried to turn around to see him, she screamed with pain and almost fainted. Shortly afterwards Kenny and Annie came in and the same thing happened again. This time we were sure that we were dealing with more than a pulled muscle and we convinced her that a trip to hospital was needed. Getting her into the car was more difficult than it had been earlier and she was suffering badly.

On arrival at Accident and Emergency we were asked to take her for an x-ray and then to come back and wait to see a doctor. We were in a tiny cubicle with Colin and me standing beside Lesley who was in a half-sitting position on a bed but in even more discomfort at this angle. When the doctor arrived with the x-ray results, I said that Lesley was very brave and didn't ever make a fuss but that he needed to know that she was in a great deal of pain, possibly because of the angle she was at. He shocked me by agreeing that she would indeed be in excruciating pain because she had broken her hip and that she was very lucky that the bone hadn't completely displaced. In my head I could see me getting her in and out of the car, up and down the stairs and in and out of the bath and the vision of the further damage that could have been caused made me pass out. This was most unlike me, the calm and capable one, and the next thing I knew was coming around and feeling very embarrassed to find myself lying on a trolley that had been squeezed into the cubicle and Colin standing between his two ladies, utterly shocked. Typical of Lesley, she was then more worried about me than herself!

She was admitted to a ward that night with surgery planned for first thing in the morning. She had to have pins and plates inserted the whole length of the femur to stabilise it and allow healing. For a few days her spirit was very low and I was worried that the reality of what a bully had done to her had caused her to become depressed. However, it turned out to be her reaction to the morphine that she was on and as soon as they changed the pain medication, she bounced back to being our usual positive girl. She broke all records for recovery and learning to walk with crutches as she was just desperate to get home.

As I had been meant to start teaching on the Monday after her weekend operation, I contacted the authorities to explain what had happened. They were very helpful and suggested that they might be able to offer me some odd days working in schools near the hospital which would allow me to be in to see Lesley first thing in the morning and then to be back before the end of afternoon visiting and free for the evening. This worked well and by the time

Lesley was due to be released I had been offered a full time position in my previous primary school in Whitburn. It was a very difficult decision to make as I had not intended taking on something full time while Lesley was still recovering. The positives were that I was literally five minutes away and could come home at lunchtime to see to Lesley's needs and would only be minutes away if she had a problem.

Colin and I talked it through with Lesley and I told the head teacher at the school about the situation. She was very keen to have me and more than willing to be accommodating until Lesley was fully fit so I returned to teach where I had started years before. Lesley would stay in bed until I came home at lunchtime and then she would move downstairs with me to support her. Sometimes her Nana and Papa would come out to spend some time with her and there were days when Colin had work to do from his home office so it worked quite well. We were fortunate that our house at that time had toilets upstairs and downstairs and she coped very well with the crutches. Her attitude, as usual in hard times, was fabulous and it wasn't long before she was back at school.

I was worried about not being there for her when she returned to the Academy but her guidance teacher made sure that she was well-supported and able to use the lift rather than the stairs to access upper floors. She got out of classes before the bells so that corridors were quiet for her and many of the children rallied around to help her. She was never openly bullied again and I hope the main protagonist realised the brutal effects of his stupid behaviour and perhaps never bullied again at all, though I may be a bit naïve there. Seemingly there had to be a court appearance for him but we were never informed of the outcome. I only know that as well as finding it very difficult to forgive him, I will never forgive myself for not doing something when the low-level bullying was taking place. You live and learn and some of the lessons are hard ones to come to terms with. The most admirable thing of it all was to find that Lesley bore no grudge and although the experience further rocked her self-esteem, she did not dwell on it or allow it to jaundice her attitudes to people. In fact, she did herself huge favours by fixing her smile in place and appearing to be fine which made people admire her spirit even more.

She needed to use two crutches for quite some time and with the hand problems she had, this was quite difficult but she was determined to cope. We decided that she needed some sort of treat to aim for during her recovery and I hit on an idea that I thought would be great for her. She adored Jason Donovan and at that time he was playing Joseph in London. I talked it over with Colin and we decided that I would take her down in the train, book an overnight stay in a hotel and take her to the theatre at night. When all the arrangements had been successfully made, we told her of the plan – and if we had offered her the moon she could not have been more impressed. The excitement gave her a real boost and she was counting down the days. Unfortunately, by the time the big day arrived, she still needed her crutches and I worried that this could make it too exhausting for her. However, adrenalin is an amazing thing and she coped with the travelling and the getting around London very well. We had to rely on taxis rather than the underground but everything worked very smoothly and we had a wonderful weekend. We hung around outside the theatre after the show in the hope of seeing Jason, but were eventually informed that he had left by a different exit.

This did not upset Lesley greatly but I knew how much she had hoped to get his autograph. When I heard that he was coming to the SECC in Glasgow sometime later to do a show I decided to write in explaining what had happened in London and asking if there was any chance of getting his autograph when we attended the show in Glasgow. I said that we had already seen him previously at the Edinburgh Playhouse and that Lesley was a huge fan since his first days of acting in Neighbours and then even more so as his singing career developed. I simply sent the letter to the SECC hoping that I would hear something back, but nothing happened.

My friend Maureen was also going to the show and had offered to pick us up and take us to Glasgow. Late morning on the day of the event I got a phone call to say that Lesley had been chosen to meet Jason before the show if we came in early. Cue utter joy and exhilaration and a panic phone call to Maureen to ask if she was free to go earlier even though she would not be able to go with us for the actual meeting. She happily agreed and was just as excited as we were. If the truth be told, Lesley was a wee bit over-awed by the occasion and I think needed more time to process what was happening. However, Jason was so relaxed and friendly when we met him that she was able to enjoy herself. There were a handful of other children each with a parent in attendance and one mother simply took over the whole event so we took a bit of a back seat to allow Lesley to simply soak up the atmosphere. She got the much desired autograph and had a photograph taken with Jason who was lovely to her, but it was all over quite quickly and we were then ushered through to our seats to enjoy the show.

Collecting autographs was to become quite an obsession for Lesley as the years went on and her collection of books hold over four hundred from the worlds of sport and entertainment. Hibernian football players were always most important for her and she needed to have every player every season – no easy task for her Dad who had to help her to complete her lists of 'most wanted'. I think Colin got to dread the news that Hibs had made a new signing because he knew exactly what that would mean! When she later developed a passion for Edinburgh Monarchs Speedway, the same situation arose with her desire to collect the riders' autographs each season. This was easy as they were always very accessible and more than willing to stop their preparations to sign the book – speedway riders do not have the egos of footballers and seem happier to relate to their fans and give them their time. Some actors, actresses and comedians made it into the books too but these were usually simply because of chance encounters though Lesley did write to a few fan clubs to ask for signed photographs of real favourites.

One of her other passions in life was music and as well as collecting autographs she began to buy CDs which ranged from sixties pop to current music bands and from ballads to rock. She had wonderful taste and genuinely enjoyed a huge range of styles and kept lists of all of her collection on a spreadsheet. She mainly kept them in zipped storage wallets organised meticulously by artist or genre though there were many filled traditional CD racks in her room too. If Lesley was in the house, there was music being played in her room and if she left the house she took her music with her. In the early years that would mean carrying a wee tape or CD player but with the advent of MP3 players it became much easier for her never to be parted from her music. Her bus journeys to work passed pleasantly with her earphones in and she loved nothing better than a long car journey where she had chosen the range of music to take with us. She would settle happily in the back seat and sing along – the length of a journey mattered little to her. Similarly, on a long flight, where Colin and I would tune into a film to pass the time, Lesley would simply seek out the music channels and settle back to enjoy whatever selection was available. For her birthday and Christmas, she would provide me with a list of anything that she desperately wanted and I could use this for any of the family who wondered if there was anything she would like. She would never ask for big presents but would be thrilled to find music CDs to add to her much-valued and enjoyed collection which rose to the high hundreds over the years.

Three years after the pins and plates were inserted in her leg, Lesley had to undergo a reversal operation. At such a young age it was not deemed advisable to leave them in place and all of the metalwork was removed in a further procedure. This one started badly. Lesley had to be in hospital by 7.30 a.m. for surgery that morning. I took her in before going to work and was told to wait till lunchtime to phone in for an update. When I made the call I was informed that Lesley still had not been taken down to theatre and that I should phone a bit later in the afternoon. I asked about afternoon visiting and was told that I should just come in as I might be able to see her for a wee while even if she was just back from surgery. The school had been happy to let me leave a bit early to be at the hospital for 3.00 p.m. so that is what I did. When I went to the ward, I saw Lesley sitting up in bed, bright as a button – but utterly starving. She still hadn't been taken for surgery and had now had nothing to eat or drink from the night before. At that, her pre-med was brought so we expected her to be taken away at any moment. However, by the time the end of the visiting hour came, she was still waiting and I went to find out what was happening. The nurses said she should be taken down within minutes and that I should go home and wait till around 6.30 p.m. to phone in and they would decide if we could see her during the evening visiting time.

I explained all of this to Lesley before I left and got back home just before 5.00 p.m. As I was unlocking the door I could hear the phone ringing and rushed to answer it. My heart was racing when I realised that it was a nurse from the hospital which made me think something had gone wrong. However, the voice was telling me that I needed to come and collect my daughter so I explained that there must be a mistake as she was having surgery. The nurse then explained that Lesley had been taken down to theatre but just as they were about to start on the operation they had realised that staff involved would have passed their allocated hours by the end of the operation – so they decided instead to postpone it! I was furious. Lesley had gone through – bravely as usual – all the worries of a procedure which had not taken place and was now being told that she would need to wait at least another week to get a theatre slot. I insisted that because of what she had been through, they should make sure that Lesley got a morning slot that would not be 'bumped' due to anything other than a genuine emergency and thankfully second time around all went well. The healing was much easier than the first time – though the stitch-line was not the neat, fine running stitch that the original surgeon had said was befitting a young lady. This time it was a line of staples the length of Lesley's leg which left a much nastier scar. This taught us a lot about the finesse and care of some doctors in comparison with others who simply got the job done – but Lesley just accepted what she had been given.

Still in her teens, Lesley gave us another fright. We had come back from holiday and had a spool of photographs to be developed. I had handed them in to the shop on Whitburn Main Street and a few days later I was going to collect them. Lesley came with me and I parked just behind the main street. She was desperate to see them and said that she would like to go to the shop so I stayed in the car. Minutes later Lesley appeared around the corner looking very pale and a bit upset. I jumped out of the car and asked what was wrong and she told me that she had tripped on the pavement and landed on her elbow. As I helped her into the car she became a bit woozy and I said that we should try to see a doctor. However, she insisted that it was probably just because she had hit the 'funny bone' and that we should just go home.

Arriving back home Lesley again bleached and became faint as soon as she moved so I made a sling and insisted on going to speak to someone at our doctor's surgery. She was again very poorly when she tried to get back into the car but then said that she thought it was feeling better in the sling and that she would probably be fine. With memories of the hip incident in the forefront of my mind, I said that I would leave her in the car and speak to the receptionist about what we should do – and it was decided that I could be given a slip to take her to Accident and Emergency for an x-ray to be on the safe side.

Lesley was worried that we were going to be wasting people's time and was quite apologetic to the young doctor who sent us to x-ray. It turned out that Lesley had a very nasty broken elbow and her whole arm, from shoulder to hand, needed to be set in plaster at an awkward angle to her body. What a shock Colin got on arriving home from work that night – not just holiday photographs to look at but a plaster to sign! Our daughter didn't ever seem to get an easy life but there were no complaints from her other than about the terrible itching inside the plaster as the weeks progressed. The biggest issues were the ones she always seemed most able to rise above and we were so proud of her positive attitude and smiling acceptance of difficult issues.

Travelling On

Relationships between Lesley and her peers were becoming more difficult for her to manage during the teen years and this impacted on things like Guide Camp weekends too. She found it very stressful to cope with other people changing plans at the last minute or messing around with the order of things in the tents. Without making any conscious decisions, we had begun to try to keep everything at home ordered, planned and quite predictive but this could not be expected of others so to balance this we had to make sure that our family holidays were more suited to Lesley.

Looking back, we could perhaps have done more if we had been aware of the autism, but we did try. If Lesley asked in the morning what we were going to do the next day, we would have been inclined to say that we would wait and see what we all felt like doing – not realising that the strained mood for the rest of the day was because we didn't take time to plan out what might be on the itinerary. In later years, our holiday plans were researched and discussed in advance and 'timetabled' as much as was possible before going, and this meant that we would have a happy trio because if Lesley was comfortable and relaxed we could all enjoy life more.

Holidays had become the highlight of the year for all of us and we relished visiting new places and experiencing all that was on offer. Lesley loved flying and even if there were flight delays, she accepted them easily as it was not a person letting her down but a notice board changing the plans. Colin and I might be annoyed but she could simply accept the inevitable and wait patiently – provided there was a cuppa on offer. She loved to get out and about on day trips as these would be planned in advance and would inform before starting exactly what the agenda for the day would be.

We met lots of people all over the world many of whom seemed very impressed with our sense of adventure and willingness to try anything in spite of Lesley's obvious difficulties. Her warm smile, almost always firmly in place for the public regardless of the situation, won her many friends and much admiration. Her beautiful manners led to her having great relationships with waiters and waitresses who were always thanked warmly and genuinely appreciated for the service they offered and we were often given a proper send-off at the end of a holiday simply because staff wanted to say goodbye to Lesley. She would be slipped extra portions of special puddings or have her drink already waiting for her on the table before we arrived for dinner. Occasionally she was even given small gifts by other holiday-makers because they had so enjoyed her company. One lady bought her a lovely necklace because she had enjoyed Lesley's company at the pool every day and said that it had made her holiday to have such good company. In Belgium when Lesley was only six years old, our waitress was Mary and she kept in touch thereafter and asked for photographs every year so that she could see how Lesley was growing up. Almost thirty years later her husband got in touch to let us know that Mary had died – and again let us know the great impression Lesley had made on her and how she had never forgotten her. A waiter in Austria ran to a bakery on our last morning because Lesley's favourite little cake hadn't arrived in time for breakfast and he wanted her to have a couple for her journey. None of this was down to Colin or me – it was Lesley's own quiet charm and genuine warmth that won people's hearts and this helped to balance the difficulties she was finding in her peer relationships as she grew up. She needed a lot of reassurance that she was a lovely person who just happened to find it difficult to cope on her own in social situations and to relate to her peer group who were maturing in ways that were leaving her behind.

She was fortunate in her Guiding life to have the opportunity to move into Ranger Guides and then to help out at a guide unit with Pamela who had been her patrol leader when she first started guides. All of this was what led to her gaining her Baden Powell award too even though parts of this were difficult for her. While at college in Bathgate, she took part in the Duke of Edinburgh Award Scheme and gained her Bronze Award. Part of this meant that she had to complete a trek in the hills and a camping night even though by this time her feet tended to cause her real problems and her hip issues also impacted on walking. She went with her feet pre-covered in Compede plasters to protect all of the worst areas and her weak ankles strapped up securely and she managed well. The highlight of the achievement for her was the fact that a celebrity was to present the award. It turned out to be Jim Leishman a Scottish football manager and the presentation was to take place at Livingston Football Stadium. As soon as we arrived, she went to ask him for his autograph and in the course of their wee chat Jim quickly realised that Lesley had a good sense of humour. She became the butt of his jokes for the whole evening which caused her equal levels of amusement and embarrassment and entertained everyone in the room! We, of course, were simply delighted and very proud parents.

The last years of Secondary School were quite difficult though Lesley did have some success with her O-level exams doing well enough in English, French and Business Studies to gain passes and completing the courses and sitting the exams in other subjects too. It was felt that rather than staying on into fifth year, it would be better for her to join the Special Education class at West Lothian College in Bathgate where it was felt her needs could best be met. We agreed to this and with a huge degree of nervousness, Lesley began a two-year course.

This was not to be a particularly successful or happy time for her though she did make some good friends. One of the boys on her course, Derek, became her partner in crime and they enjoyed some meals out together for a number of years before drifting apart when their adult lives went down different paths. There were also a few members of staff who became real favourites of Lesley's and she kept in touch with them after leaving. One of the lecturers, Elaine, always sent Christmas cards with updates about her own growing family. Lesley loved to help Ann in the office and was further drawn to her on finding that her husband, Alex, was the head of security at Hibs. Colin and Lesley got to know Alex well and were devastated when he died and Lesley was very proud for us to attend his huge funeral. She kept in touch with Ann even after Ann moved to England and never forgot her kindness and support during the college years.

There were work-placements offered during the course but not much effort seemed to go into finding Lesley anything suitable. Bearing in mind that she had no fingers, short arms and limited mobility and dexterity, it did not seem practical to have sent her to be a chambermaid in a hotel where she was meant to wear rubber gloves to clean toilets – no gloves possible for Lesley of course – or to strip and make up beds. Other work offered was with a company which packaged earphones for planes into small bags and another where steering wheel gloves for cars had to be packaged at speed. Lesley's reviews were obviously quite negative with these employers saying that she would not be suitable for them as her work was too slow. She had a couple of shop placements but although she coped better with these, she was unhappy because she felt that most people coming into the shops who didn't know her stared and talked about her. These experiences further eroded Lesley's already diminishing self-esteem and confidence and at the end of the two year course I was asked to go in to discuss their recommendations for the future.

Lesley had always said that she wanted office work but we were told that there was only one place that they thought could be suitable for Lesley and it was in an out-of-the-way area in Edinburgh. It was a café staffed by young people who had difficulties in finding open employment and we were told that an appointment had been made for Lesley and me to go and meet the manager. We duly organised the trip and planned it as if Lesley was making her own way there. We had to get a bus from Whitburn to Bathgate, a train to Edinburgh, a bus to the right area of the city and then a walk to the placement. It took us hours and Lesley was pretty exhausted by the time we arrived.

Almost as soon as we were introduced to the manager I knew that it was not going to be an option – and the manager's face was telling me that she felt the same. The duties were to chop vegetables for soup, prepare salads and sandwiches and to wash dishes in huge, deep sinks wearing heavy duty rubber gloves. The lady kept stressing that time was important and that the jobs had to be done quickly and efficiently so that they could keep things in the café running smoothly. These were not going to be tasks that Lesley could do quickly – if at all - and we had to bring this out into the open. It turned out that the manager had not been told of

Lesley's hand problems and she was very embarrassed that we had to raise the issue ourselves. She took us for a cuppa and apologised that our trip had been such a waste of time – but I think there was simply a great deal of relief for Lesley in finding that she was not going to be expected to travel for hours both ways every day to cope with work that was beyond her physical ability. We simply had to draw a line under the college experience and write it off.

I was then left with Lesley having no future prospects and had to find something else that would keep her involved and stimulated. Her desire had always been to be doing some sort of office work and I was able to find a place for her with Lothian Training that would further develop her office and computer skills. This was very successful at first and the manager there kept her busy with the course work and then by also doing some work for him out-with her training hours. She was happy, stimulated and felt valued and a real part of things. Sadly, as time went on there was a change of management and Lesley did not have the same opportunities or successes. This led to her becoming attention seeking again and moodier and life became quite difficult. Eventually we realised that she had come to the end of the benefits of the training with nothing further on offer which would meet her needs and another search was necessary to find a new purpose for her.

The only highlight at this time was Lesley's 18th birthday celebrations. In spite of her having become very self-conscious in her teenage years she decided that she would like to have a party for her birthday and we were happy to plan this with her. We hired a hall in the Hilcroft Hotel in Whitburn and booked the disco and arranged a finger food buffet supper. Then we began to draw up a guest list in readiness for sending out invitations. Lesley stunned us with a couple of the requests for guests she would like to be there. One was the consultant surgeon at Canniesburn who had taken over from Ian Jackson and had been in charge of Lesley's case for many years – Professor Moos. The other was Dougie Cromb who at that time was the Hibs chairman and who always talked to Colin and Lesley on match-days. Lesley wanted to invite him and his wife even though she had never even met Lotte. We explained to Lesley that these were people who were kind to her and always pleased to see her, but that this did not mean that they would consider themselves to be in her circle of friends. We further said that they would not know anyone else at the party, that Whitburn was miles away from their homes and that although it was a lovely thought, these were people who would not come.

Lesley said that she understood and appreciated what we were saying but wondered if it would still be all right to invite them because she considered them to be like friends and she wanted them to know that. How could we disagree with her thinking and her generosity of spirit? Other people invited were family and friends and we knew that the hall would be well-filled if most people were able to make it so all of the invitations were duly posted. The first two replies arrived very quickly – and to the utter amazement of Colin and me, these first acceptances came from

Dougie and Lotte Cromb and Professor Moos! This says a great deal about my lovely daughter and the relationships she formed with people she felt comfortable with regardless of the social boundaries other people might be influenced by.

As it turned out, everyone invited came and a wonderful night took place. Colin and I are not really party people and we were worried about the responsibility of making sure that people were having a good time but we needn't have been concerned. Family members from two-year old cousins to grandparents loved the occasion with the two youngest cousins particularly enjoying the buffet and the dancing. Lesley's Uncle Kenny hired a 'Mr Blobby' costume as a surprise due to Lesley loving 'Noel's House Party' on television at that time – but ended up terrifying his own wee daughter, Claire! There were tables full of young people who were Lesley's friends from childhood or college days. There were lots of our family friends with their own children who had grown up with Lesley. Lesley had invited Martha and Biff her Guide leaders and as they were Hibs fans it proved a very successful match to sit them with Dougie and Lotte – a real treat for them to socialise with the Chairman! Lesley was very fond of my first boss in teaching, Miss McGill or 'Aunt Chrissie' to Lesley and of course she had been invited and came wearing a beautiful deep blue velvet off-the-shoulder evening gown – and she was seated with my parents and was joined by Professor Moos when he arrived. They hit it off immediately and talked all night. It turned out that the attendance of the professor was even more to be admired as his mother had died that week. However, he came to us before he left and said that it had been an honour and a privilege to attend particularly to see one of his patients surrounded by friends and simply enjoying life. Ordinarily all he saw was the patient for surgery or review and the occasion had given him a great deal of delight and pride that his involvement had played a part in Lesley becoming the lovely adult who was celebrating that night.

Any worries or nervousness about the success of the occasion soon faded for Colin and me and we were simply able to enjoy it all with Lesley surrounded by people who cared about her and who were delighted to share her big night. We had wondered if we should make a speech during the evening and neither of us was very keen to do so. Colin felt that he was likely to be too emotional to see it through and I was nervous about standing in front of everyone. However, we also thought that we needed to thank people for coming and acknowledge that this was a bit more than a usual eighteenth due to all that had happened in Lesley's life. I opted to write a poem so that I could make a simple statement of thanks to everyone for their attendance and gifts and then just read the poem. This worked well and there were more than a few tears in the hall – and not just from Colin!

Happy Birthday Lesley

On a bright and frosty morning 18 years ago this week
A baby girl was born one Sunday and her future looked gey bleak.
She had far too many problems for one poor wee mite to thole
And her eyes were wise and worried like the windows to her soul.
She was in an incubator - the doctor worried about her heart
But they allowed her Mum to hold her hand and love grew from the start.
Her name had been chosen - Lesley – but now to help her cope
A middle name was added, a simple one, just Hope.
It was all they had to go on in those long hours filled with dread
And it made them focus on the future, to hope for better days ahead.
They rushed her to Edinburgh with her Dad and Papa giving chase
A high speed journey which started Lesley tackling life at fastest pace
Her Nana helped her Dad with phone calls to tell friends about her plight
Her Mum was left behind at Bangour, missing her in the night.
At 'Sick Kids' hospital they were worried and kept her in the incubator,
But this wee Lesley was a fighter and was home just one week later!
There followed days of fun and laughter, but other times as well
The good days were real treasures but the bad days straight from Hell.
Days of pain and hurt and worry spent in hospital, not home
But those who really loved her made sure she never coped alone.

Happy Birthday Lesley

Lesley made it through the bad times, as a patient she has no equal
And I'm glad to say the story has a very happy sequel.
She's abseiled down a rock-face and she's even done free-fall
Completed Duke of Edinburgh Bronze, 15-mile expedition and all
She has mountain biked and kayak canoed – though she fell in at the side
And she gained her Baden Powell award, the highest for a Guide.
Her biggest love is football; she's a Hibee through and through
Even though her Mum has tried so hard to turn her nose blue!
She has filled our lives with love, even through those teenage years
When we'd have the kind of rows that would only end in tears
She has cared for other people, sensed their hurt and shared their pain
What she's been through in life tested her again and again.
She's an adult now, our baby, and though we wouldn't like to boast
We think that Lesley Hope McRobb is most worthy of a toast.
So please stand and raise your glasses as we celebrate tonight
Happy birthday to a daughter who has turned out 'Just right'!

After much investigation – and weeks passing where Lesley was simply spending her time at home – I found out about the Prince's Trust Course. Not all aspects of the course suited her but she made the best of it and tried hard to do all that was expected of her – including taking part in an end of course stage performance for families, friends and other guests to attend and where she was awarded her certificate. The featured song was 'I am what I am' and Lesley loved the song anyway which helped her to have the confidence to take part. She had her own role in the performance and carried it off well with lots of humour and we were extremely proud of her. Considering her lack of confidence and low self-esteem it was a major achievement to get up on stage to sing and dance with the other course participants.

The best bit of her time on the course was when she had to carry out a work-experience placement. She was allocated to Disability West Lothian who were then based in Bathgate and she loved her couple of weeks with them. On leaving, Andrew, the manager, told her that if she did not have any other work offers at the end of the course they would be delighted to have her as a volunteer. She already had experience of volunteering as she had helped at Radio Grapevine at St John's Hospital for a couple of years one day a week and was listed with the local volunteer service. When she took up her placement with Disability West Lothian she earned herself further certificates in recognition of the number of hours she had given as a volunteer and this was again a great boost to her feeling of self-worth.

Over time, as well as becoming a valued member of the team, Lesley formed strong friendships with some of the other volunteers, many of whom had their own problems to cope with. This was to become Lesley's comfort zone where she felt accepted, valued and part of a team. She didn't ever treat it as anything other than 'her work' and although she was not paid a penny she gave it more commitment than many career people. She was always on time, willing to do anything and was virtually never off. She would convince me that being under the weather was no reason not to go in and her high work ethic was exceptional. She would go off for the bus regardless of weather conditions and would only get upset if a bus didn't turn up making her arrive late.

She benefitted from her involvement in lots of ways. She was in receipt of benefits by this time and she felt that by working four days a week she was earning them and this gave her a sense of pride. She loved the office tasks and became greatly admired for her computer skills. She learned a lot from the staff about being part of a team in the working world and realised that she had a lot to offer. Her confidence grew because of the development of friendships with her peers, something that had been lost to her for a while. Her life became quite full and she took part in a range of activities out-with the office setting.

She had always gone swimming with her friend Leigh but they began to have another night in the week when they met up to simply socialise. She joined a group through her work and they would go out for meals, go to shows and concerts and even for a few weekend breaks away. She had football with her Dad which she adored and eventually she also developed the love of Speedway that her Dad and I had. Although her life had limitations she was enjoying so much more than she had during her teenage years and we were thrilled for her. Some weeks were almost busier than she could cope with and she would call herself 'Mrs Never In!'.

All of this gave a balance that had been missing and which we were all glad of when there were the inevitable bad times. Further major surgery had taken place in her mid-teens to do more restructuring of her face and skull. This had been a very difficult time for us all as Lesley was very ill after the operation and didn't regain full consciousness for days. She had lost a great deal of blood needing transfusions and was very poorly. We had a few days of thinking that we were losing her though thankfully when she did come around she made progress very quickly and was her usual brave and cheerful self. Colin and I felt sure that this was the final big cranio-facial surgery and were very relieved when we got her back home to recover and get her life back. Even then it was a difficult time due to Lesley having her mouth all wired together and only being able to have liquidised food – and for someone who loved food the way she did, this was major! However, as usual, she put up with all that was involved though the speech therapy in Glasgow wasn't a great success. Her mouth and jaw structure had been changed so much that she was referred for specialist speech therapy to help her to form sounds in a new way but it is very hard to 'unlearn' something. Eventually we decided that we would simply work hard at home rather than trailing in regularly for the sessions with the therapist and good progress was made.

She got rid of most of the wiring but needed a lot of work on the teeth to get them into better alignment. She had the benefit of newly developed types of wires to anchor them in place but this also meant many visits to the Dental Hospital in Glasgow to have them adjusted. Sometimes a length of wire would 'spring' and begin to cut the inside of Lesley's cheeks which was excruciating. We had wax-like material to press onto the wire to give temporary protection until we could get in to have things adjusted and this happened regularly for quite some time. The upside of this was that she was eventually under the care of Mr Gillgrass and she loved her visits to see him because he had such an easy manner and Lesley enjoyed their friendly banter. In time there was just a little retaining wire attached to the back of her top teeth and the visits became annual formalities rather than regular chores.

Following a routine check-up at Canniesburn a few years later with other options mentioned by the surgeon, Lesley wanted to have further work done - against our better judgement. Our memories of the last time were still very fresh and we discussed with her the risks involved against any possible benefits. However, Lesley was adamant that she wanted a better nose and cheek bones and improvements on her forehead and jaw-line and she decided that she wanted it to go ahead. In the early years when the operations were to save her life or to improve her breathing and therefore her general health, the decisions were easier to make but Colin and I were extremely worried and got more and more anxious as the date drew near. We knew that again it would be at least ten or twelve hours of anaesthetic with all the risks that involved and we remembered only too well the worries of the first few days the last time.

On the day, which like the others seemed to last for a week, we waited for news with trepidation. That evening the surgeon eventually came to tell us that things had to be rushed a bit at the end as Lesley was becoming poorly and our fears seemed to be proved correct. We were taken to her bedside as soon as she was brought from recovery and walked towards her with heavy hearts. As usual, her face and head were swollen badly with bruising already showing and she was very pale and unmoving with her eyes closed. However as soon as I touched her, her eyes flew open and she said 'Was there any mail for me this morning Mum?' We were quite simply stunned and couldn't believe that she was fully awake and aware and being nosy about there being any get well cards for her – which there were, much to her delight!

Recovery this time was much less fraught in all ways but the outcomes were not as good as we had hoped and Lesley herself was a bit disappointed. This time she decided for herself that she didn't want to have any further work done and seemed more able to resign herself to accept the person she was rather than always hoping for improvements. It was never about a lack of courage to face difficulties or pain but more about coming to terms with what had been achieved and accepting that the best had already been done – and this took a level of bravery that only those who have gone through similar experiences could possibly understand.

She did at one time ask her GP to refer her to have work carried out on her hands. As a little girl she had completely floored me one day when she asked when her hands would start to grow like everyone else's. That was a hard thing to take as we thought she had understood that her condition was permanent and were a bit shocked to discover that she hadn't taken that in at all. Visiting hospital and having doctors examine her hands and take x-rays had obviously not led to her realising that her hands really were different. I explained to her as simply as I could that her hands were just made that way and that the doctors couldn't do anything to help because her hands were too small – and as a child she accepted this. If she asked why her hands were different we would simply say that it was because she was special and had just been made that way.

It turned out that now as an adult some of her friends had been asking her why she didn't get her fingers separated – they were sure this would be an easy thing to have done, not realising that Lesley's hands weren't simply webbed but the bones were totally fused. As it had been back in early childhood that we had been told that surgery was not considered to be an option, Lesley had no memory of any discussions and thought that we had just neglected this and the GP agreed to refer her for a second opinion.

I must admit to being quite taken aback that Lesley had arranged this – the first I knew of it was when an appointment came in for her to see a specialist yet she wouldn't normally go to the doctor with something as simple as a throat infection without me present. I did explain all that had been said in the past but I don't think Lesley really believed me as she had no recollection of these discussions or evaluations. We went to hospital and photographs and x-rays were taken first so that the consultant could evaluate things before seeing her. Sadly, for Lesley, he expressed strong reservations about doing any work on her hands and asked her why she wanted to consider surgery at this point in her life. She told him that she wanted to have hands that looked like other people's hands, which was very hard to hear.

Without even pausing for thought the doctor explained that there was no way this could ever happen. He said that he could separate the little finger on each hand but that if there was no control of them after the surgery they may later have to be removed if they were getting caught in things and being injured and damaged. He discussed options about trying to improve the shape of her thumbs but again felt that this could result in her losing the strength of the grip she had with them and therefore she would be worse off. He also explained that she would have no use of her hands for some time with splinting being necessary and only one hand being worked on at a time. By the time he had gone over all of this, Lesley was looking very upset and told him that she had made a mistake as she thought it would be easy to improve them. She didn't want to risk being worse off and was not actually complaining about the restrictions on manual dexterity that she experienced, she simply thought her hands could look more normal.

The consultant was very compassionate and reassured her that she had been right to find out her options and if she should ever want to discuss things further he would happily see her again.

When we left she broke down completely and admitted that she hadn't believed us when we told her that we had already investigated it all thoroughly and had dealt with a top plastic surgeon from Edinburgh who had told us that it was the size of Lesley's hands which made any intervention too difficult and risky. A lot of cuddles and reassurance were needed that day but I think Lesley was finally able to draw a line under surgical intervention and learn to ignore people who said 'it's great what they can do nowadays' without having any idea of what would actually be involved or of what could be the result. This was a hard lesson but maybe one that needed to be learned the hard way.

Adult Life

It was probably around this time that I began to realise that as well as Lesley's obvious problems, autism would explain a lot of her difficulties in coping with life. Obsessions and compulsions have been mentioned previously and some of these were harder to ignore than others. When she got a mobile phone she began to obsess about texting and sadly she bombarded her former Guider until she was on the point of reporting her as a nuisance. We hadn't known about it and thought that as soon as we had explained how wrong it was, all would be well. Obsessions are not that easy to deal with and the poor girl had to come back to us within a week of first speaking to tell us that it hadn't stopped in spite of all of Lesley's promises. This forced me to take her phone away for a wee while and to make her understand that this could be a criminal act to try to make her see the seriousness of the matter – not to mention that she was losing a caring friend because of it.

Although we didn't ask about a formal diagnosis at this time, we were trying to use autism-friendly strategies at home to help Lesley to cope with life. However, we were not in control of other people and sadly when their actions upset Lesley, she kept it bottled up until she was at home and then rages could erupt without us having any idea of the cause. For years it was only ever me that was subjected to these rages but eventually Colin would also get some of the backlash. We could regularly have hours on end of Lesley storming backwards and forwards through the house, banging doors and muttering, but completely unable to verbalise her problems or discuss what had upset her. Sometimes she would inform us that she was moving out and she would grab bags and begin to pack her belongings, only to later spend hours putting everything away again. This was very hard to live with and it wasn't ever possible to predict when things would blow up.

Tragically, if it all built up to a very high level, Lesley could also become violent and she had the strength of ten men when adrenalin was surging and the rage drove her on with no conscious thinking about what she was doing. It could take anything from a few hours to a day or more for her to totally calm down and then she would be distraught at her behaviour – even though lots of it was not in her memory. There were times when she would see bruises on me and ask me – in shocked tones – what had happened to me only to be devastated to find that she had caused them. This was heart-breaking as Lesley was innately a gentle, kind and caring person who would not ever have wanted to cause anyone any pain – least of all me, who she adored. We would talk and talk about ways to recognise the early signs of her rising anger and we came up with many things she could try to do to 'nip it in the bud' but it just didn't work.

I tried a card system with pictures that showed her mood so that she could simply leave a card in view to tell us that she wasn't coping but although she thought it was a good idea when we discussed it calmly, it didn't work in the real situations. The episodes were difficult for Colin and me as a couple too. I wouldn't let Colin intervene physically in case Lesley got hurt but that would mean he had to watch as she took her anger out on me and he found it unbearable and impossible to cope with at times. Only the love we all had for each other kept us together because sometimes it would have been very easy to throw in the towel and walk away. There is no magic wand when dealing with the anxieties caused by autistic reactions to things in life and we knew that help was required. Maybe to other people it appeared that if Lesley could control her feelings in public places she should also be able to cope within our home but it doesn't work that way. The effort that went in to her keeping things together in the outside world was utterly exhausting and the build-up of emotions was like trying to keep the lid on a volcano that was already erupting – it had to happen and sadly we had to deal with the outpouring of bottled up anger.

We had asked for a referral to speak to someone who might be able to help Lesley in ways that we weren't aware of but we had to wait for a very long time for her referral to be dealt with. Perhaps if we had already asked for a formal diagnosis of autism things would have moved more quickly though there would still not have been a 'quick fix'. She eventually had a few sessions with a psychiatric counsellor who advised her to keep a record of how she felt physically and emotionally before, during and after an episode. We drew up a table on the computer with the headings he advised and talked through the kind of things he was looking for. However, Lesley would simply insist that I tell her what she should put in it and got angry when I said that it had to be her own thoughts and not my observations. Unfortunately, she wasn't able to recall the kinds of things she was being asked to note. She would go back each week and the counsellor would see her on her own while I waited outside. She would then come out and tell me that he thought she was doing very well because she had told him that her week had been good and that she had only maybe shouted a wee bit but not got very angry – yet I had the bruises to tell a very different story and she had the dreadful regrets of more awful incidents some weeks.

She appeared to be doing so well that she was quickly discharged and Colin and I were left wondering why we had bothered in the first place. With no improvements as the months went on, we all went together to see a GP to ask if medication might be an option to help Lesley to remain a bit calmer when there had been things in her day that had caused her to get overly wound up. Sadly, having bared our souls which was very difficult to do as we had kept all of the bad times very private over the years, the doctor simply told us that medication was not an option and that Lesley should simply imagine herself in a nice place if she began to feel angry and this would help her to stay calm. If she didn't stay calm, we should consider having her charged! He then said that Lesley was an adult and that we should leave the room as Lesley was his patient and he would discuss things with her alone. We were shocked and devastated and when Lesley came out a few minutes later she said that he had just told her that she would need to try harder not to get angry. I despair when I wonder if other people are sometimes left feeling as bad as we felt that night.

For over twenty years we had simply coped with everything that Lesley's condition had thrown at us, whether it was social, emotional, physical, mental, behavioural or medical and we had loved her throughout and made sure all her needs were met. For the first time we had admitted that life was becoming increasingly difficult to cope with and that we felt Lesley was suffering badly from the effects of these rages as well as the regrets she had afterwards at her treatment of us – and we were simply told to leave. Due to this treatment it was many years before I was again willing to speak to a GP about Lesley's moods and rages and this is something that I deeply regret as she was later helped considerably.

When Lesley and I went to see a different GP some years later, the reaction could not have been more different. He instantly tuned in and asked Lesley and me questions about the sort of things that triggered the rages. Lesley was able to tell him that it might be people changing plans at the last minute or someone saying she had made a mistake at work or the bus being late arriving or the rain coming on when the forecast had been for a dry day. He discussed the fact that she only 'blew up' at home and she said that she tried to keep it all inside her but she could only manage that until she was in her own house and then the smallest thing was the last straw for her and she just lost control.

I explained that we wondered if there were perhaps tablets that we could keep in the house so that if Lesley could identify quickly enough that she was feeling very angry, she could take one and try to avert a full rage. The doctor agreed that there were indeed such options but he then went on to explain to Lesley – in the most compassionate way – that she was suffering from heightened anxiety levels all day every day and that no one could tolerate such conditions without really suffering. He told her that it was very wrong to be violent but that he understood why it was happening and could help to take the edge of her anxiety levels by prescribing tablets that she would take every day.

My worry then was that she was being 'doped' every day just to avert the bad days but he explained that it was very unlikely that we would even notice any difference in Lesley other than keeping her a bit calmer in general and therefore not over reacting to minor incidents. She would be started on the lowest dose which could then be increased if required and a second prescription would be for tablets for use on 'bad days' only. He talked it all through carefully and checked that Lesley understood and agreed and that I was happy with the planned intervention. He also said that he would see her again soon to make sure she was well and to monitor her progress. On leaving he stood and shook my hand and wished us well and I could have hugged him as I struggled not to sob with relief.

Lesley cried when we later told Colin all that had happened and said that she wished we had seen him years before because then maybe she would have been better to us. We reassured her that, although we all knew it was wrong to treat us badly, we understood and always loved her and maybe with the right medication things would improve.

It would be wrong for me to imply that everything was perfect after that but the difference was immense. The tablets did not have any bad side-effects for Lesley and within a week or two we were noticing a big change. There is no doubt that our daughter was happier and calmer and much less likely to over react to little things. There were still occasional times when rages blew up but on the whole these were the result of bigger issues and sometimes the use of the additional medication brought things under control quite quickly. Over time, the daily tablets needed to be increased in strength when it was obvious that they were no longer doing enough but the doctor had explained that this could happen and that there were plenty of options to increase the dose and the number of tablets taken in a day to get the right balance. We found that it was necessary to spread them out at three intervals in the day to get best results and this stabilised the anxiety levels quite well. We also learned that if there was a very big event planned which would cause Lesley heightened anxiety, she would take one of the other tablets that morning and this worked well for her.

There were, of course, some events that just happened and caused problems for Lesley which couldn't have been anticipated and which still wound her up enough to cause her to react but these lessened greatly to a level that was bearable – even if still upsetting at the time. Lesley was extremely grateful that someone understood without judging her or simply telling her to deal with it. She had tried so hard for so long and now life was kinder for her – and us.

Over the years I had developed an 'alter ego' character called – to give her Sunday name - Samantha Josephine Farquharson McRobb who had 'joined' us having supposedly lost her own family. She was often used to diffuse difficult situations before they got out of hand. Sami Jo was a confident, out-going, rather cheeky little girl with a huge sense of fun and an engaging, positive attitude. We even 'saw' her as a wee blonde girl with bunches and wearing dungarees! She was always up for adventures and didn't mind getting things wrong or getting into trouble. I had a voice for Sami and would sometimes manage to get Sami to talk to Lesley when it appeared that there was a problem that she wasn't managing to tell me about. It didn't always work but it was a useful tool to try as a first step towards getting a problem sorted out. Sami also had great ideas for things she would like to do at times when Lesley was reluctant to come up with any options for doing things in her free time and she would take the suggestions that Sami made and consider them even if she was actually being a wee bit snappy or withdrawn with Colin and me. It seemed to help Lesley to get things off her chest through talking to this 'non-person' and if she approached me by saying 'Sami' rather than 'Mum', it let me know that she was feeling a bit fragile and needing to communicate something that was a bit of an issue for her to deal with. It may sound silly but it did help in our household and anything that eased Lesley's emotional or communication issues was welcome. Sami gave us lots of laughs in our house.

Lesley was well used to coping with physical pain and seldom ever moaned. She would simply ask me if I would put some Compede plasters on her foot – and this would be the first I knew of a horrible blister or a bruised or grazed area where shoes had rubbed because her feet had swollen. Her hip regularly gave her considerable pain and her ankles needed supports put on every day but still by night time they would be very swollen and sore. Her nails and ears needed a lot of attention too and she would simply come to me and ask if 'Nurse McRobb' was free to help her. She accepted that this was her lot and just got on with it. It was the emotional health that had been destroying her and it was great to see her happier and calmer and more able to get the best from life – and to become a bit more like Sami Jo!

For Lesley, the best things in life were football, music, speedway, puzzle books, Inside Soap magazine, meals out and holidays. She subscribed to a puzzle book which arrived every month and which she enjoyed completing at night while she watched television. She also took them on holiday with her and this allowed her to pass her time happily while travelling or chilling in a hotel. There were only certain television programmes that she really enjoyed and some of these were 'analysed' in the Inside Soap magazine which she also subscribed to. This allowed her to be in the know before me in relation to storylines in Coronation Street which we both loved. She would whisper things to Colin about upcoming events and then wait for me to find out what was happening as the stories developed. She loved the fact that she knew before me and got a lot of pleasure out of the fact that Colin, who wasn't really interested, knew about the big stories ahead of me too! She loved all the MasterChef programmes and was devastated when Wild at Heart finished as it was a particular favourite – so much so that she bought the DVD set so that she could continue to watch episodes at her leisure.

I've already mentioned her love of music and her collection of CDs. Supporting Hibernian Football Club wasn't always easy if results were poor but along with her Dad she was passionate about the game from 1991 onwards and utterly loyal to her team. She experienced many cup semi-final and final disappointments at Hampden Park before eventually seeing Hibs win the League Cup in great style in 2007. Following the match, Colin and Lesley went straight back through to Edinburgh to the stadium in Leith to await the victorious arrival of the team to their home stadium and to be part of the joyous celebrations. They were simply overjoyed and it took days for them to return to earth! This was Colin's dream come true – for the two of them to be together and see their team winning a trophy. Colin always says it is his happiest day with Lesley and comparable to the way I felt about her day as the Rainbow Fairy Queen.

It wasn't until the speedway season of 2003 that she really got into speedway and became a fanatical Monarchs supporter. Previously she had only attended one or two matches a season and couldn't adjust to the noise and having to stand throughout the meeting. In 2003 she came for a few meetings in a row and found that as soon as she had more understanding of the scoring and the rules, she began to enjoy the action and excitement. She was quickly hooked and in fact I think eventually if she had been forced to choose between attending football or speedway, the Mighty Monarchs would have won – not that this choice was ever forced on her.

Part of her enjoyment of the Friday nights at Armadale came from the banter of the crowd around us. We were a very diverse group brought together simply because of a love of speedway, a passion for supporting the Monarchs and the coincidence of where we had chosen to stand. Over the years, mere acquaintance developed into friendships and there was always plenty of talking and joking between heats. Lesley loved this – an intense minute of excitement and adrenalin during a race followed by five minutes to relax, discuss the race and the riders and catch up with the news with those around us.

She certainly chose the right season to become a fan because for the first time in their history, the Monarchs won the league that year, coming out on top against teams from as far afield as the south of England. The celebrations were immense and Lesley loved being part of it all. She was to see other trophies being won in later years but nothing would compare with the delight of that first league title and the celebrations with the riders, the management and all of the fans.

The other benefit to come from her enjoyment of attending meetings was her growing friendship with Lynnette, a young lady just a year younger than herself who came with her Dad and stood beside us. They only had speedway in common to begin with but Lesley admired Lynnette's speedway knowledge and they also quickly realised that they had a shared sense of humour. They became great friends and would phone and text each other and meet up for lunches or coffees often. It was great for her to have another close friend with a shared interest in common.

We wanted Lesley to have interests and friendships which were not dependent on us and we were delighted when she went out and about with friends from work or with Leigh and Lynnette. However most of the time she was relying on us to organise things and to take and collect her and this impacted on her feelings of independence. When the local newspaper had an article about Befrienders we discussed this with Lesley to see if she had any interest in joining the scheme. She was a wee bit nervous about it but thought it might be worth finding out more so we applied.

Audrey, the lady who organised it, came out to meet us all and to discuss the kind of things Lesley would enjoy doing with a Befriender and she said that she thought it would be a very good idea for Lesley. She went ahead and made the arrangements to identify a volunteer Befriender – and Lesley could not have been more fortunate to be teamed up with Jillian.

They instantly hit it off even though both of them were probably rather nervous about how it would all work. It was Jillian's first time of being linked with a possible Befriendee and we admired her for it. She was only slightly older than Lesley and they discovered quickly that they both had similar tastes in music, enjoyed ten pin bowling – and more importantly, they both loved going out for a meal. They arranged to have their first night out with Jillian saying she was happy to come in her car to pick Lesley up and bring her back home afterwards so that their outings would never be dependent on Colin or me being available for lifts.

We were all quite nervous on the first night but this proved to have been a very pointless waste of nervous energy. Lesley came home on a high having thoroughly enjoyed her night and saying that Jillian was great company and they had never stopped talking. It quickly developed into far more than a befriending relationship, they genuinely became good friends and enjoyed each other's company and this was great for Lesley's self-esteem. They went to theatre shows, bowling, the cinema, enjoyed meals in various restaurants or just had a run in the car for an ice cream on a good day. They also attended group events organised by Audrey and her team where they had trips to the seaside or took part in bowling tournaments – which they often won much to Lesley's delight. When she came home with her first trophy for ten pin bowling we celebrated as if she had won an Olympic gold! Ten years of going out every three or four weeks followed and Lesley was delighted to be told that in recognition of the success of their pairing she was being awarded a certificate and Jillian was to be recognised with a presentation and gift to show everyone's admiration. Jillian herself told us that she didn't see some of her friends nearly as often as she saw Lesley and that if the befriending side of things stopped, nothing would change for her and Lesley and this meant a great deal to us all.

Holidays

The other great passion for Lesley was her love of travelling and holidays with The Three Musketeers on Tour! As we became better off financially, the early holidays spent in caravans in the UK or cheap hotels in Spain or Belgium made way for trips further afield. Lesley had no real concept of what she achieved with her travels around the world – if I had suggested a week in Banff, Scotland she would have appreciated it just as much as an announcement that we were heading for Banff, Canada – which we did! I eventually bought a poster showing a world map and put it up on the wall behind my bedroom door. Every time we went to a new country we would put stickers on the world map so that Lesley could plot her journeys and see at a glance how far she had travelled. It was a wonderful visual image and a reminder of the experiences we had enjoyed around the world.

When a holiday was being discussed I would do all the research once we had decided on a destination and we would plan as much as was possible in advance. The first really big undertaking came about due to us talking about our Silver Wedding Anniversary which followed Lesley's 21st birthday. She had no desire for a party for this birthday – and likewise we had no plans for a party for our anniversary. I asked where in the world Lesley would choose to visit if there were no limits on the options and she immediately said that she would love to go to Australia. On hearing this, Colin replied that this would be his choice too if it was at all possible.

I was initially taken aback as I hadn't ever thought of going so far and as Colin could only have two weeks at any one time off work I doubted that it would even be a feasible option. I was happy to look into it and soon discovered a wonderful package that could easily be put together if Colin could have an extra three days tagged on to his annual leave. His company agreed, particularly as he explained it was to celebrate a major anniversary and we eagerly planned the trip. We were going to be flying around the world which sounded like something only the rich and famous would do and our excitement grew as the big day drew nearer.

We had to travel from Edinburgh to London and then on to Australia after a stop in Singapore. After refuelling in Darwin we arrived in Cairns where we had a wonderful few days taking in the rainforest and the Great Barrier Reef. Lesley got to hold a koala called Basil and instantly fell in love! She always liked to buy herself a t-shirt depicting the places she had visited and she immediately bought one with a koala on the front. We moved on to Ayres Rock for a couple of nights and had an amazing outdoor sunset dinner seeing the sun set on Uluru and The Olgas. Then it was time to head for Sydney, a city we adored and where we headed to the Blue Mountains and a wonderful wildlife park for more koalas, kangaroos and more wonderful Aussie animals than we could have dreamed of seeing let alone touching. We had the amazing experience of having a meal at the top of the AMP Tower where the restaurant constantly revolves giving ever changing views of the city. We tried food that we had never been offered before such as camel, crocodile and emu and all of it was delicious.

Our next port of call should have been Fiji but sadly a civil war denied us this opportunity and we were offered Los Angeles instead. This didn't quite equate to Fiji but we still made the most of our time there and enjoyed visiting many of the local areas like Santa Monica, Hollywood, Beverley Hills, Venice Beach and Marina Del Rey. Probably Lesley's highlight during these few days was discovering the stars on the pavement of the Walk of Fame outside the Chinese Theatre and finding Elton John's star.

On the return journey we arrived back in London and then boarded our flight for Edinburgh. Imagine Lesley's delight when she noticed Nick Nairn the Scottish chef boarding behind us. At that time, he frequently appeared on 'Ready, Steady, Cook' on television and this was one of her favourite programmes with the larger-than-life Ainslie Harriot fronting the show and Nick one of her most enjoyed guest chefs. He was wearing his tartan trousers and as it turned out he was returning to Scotland after filming some of the episodes. Lesley wondered if it would be in order for her to ask for his autograph and we told her that she could approach him but not to be upset if he turned her down. She understood that celebrities probably got really fed up of being disturbed. It was quite a while before she returned to us, beaming from ear to lug, because Nick had asked where she had been and wanted to know all about her trip. Needless to say, he could have had no idea of how much his lovely friendly manner meant to Lesley and he went up in our esteem because of it.

Possibly the best thing to come out of this holiday was the fact that long haul travelling had not phased Lesley in any way – in fact she slept most of the time on planes or simply relaxed and enjoyed the music on offer. Indeed, she was much more laid-back in her attitude than her parents and we learned a lot from her. The success of the trip allowed us to develop our adventurous spirits and gave free rein to my desire to see the world and experience as many peoples and cultures as possible.

There followed not just holidays but adventures all over the world where we enjoyed different cultures, customs, religions and cuisines and met many wonderful local people. Lesley would always bring back little souvenirs for her friends and postcards to be displayed in the kitchen at her work. No one could have grudged her the experiences she had but I'm sure there were many people who would have loved the opportunities to see the sights we saw. Lesley would never brag about any of it, she would simply tell people where she was going and her attitude in the run-up to the holiday was no different whether it was Cornwall or Canada.

Not only did we travel to far-flung places, we also tried to take in as much as possible of the area while we were there and to learn about the people and their way of life. We followed the Australia trip by confidently embracing any opportunity that appealed to all of us. Usually it was down to me to come up with a selection of possible places to visit and we would then all vote for the one that appealed most at the time. I think Australia was the only time when Lesley came up with the original idea but she did have opinions to offer on my other suggestions – though I think she would have been happy to go almost anywhere. She took the travelling in her stride as long as she knew the itinerary and could be geared up for whatever was involved. In her favour, she had a wonderful ability to grab a sleep anywhere, anytime, whether on buses, trains or planes and this sustained her during long-haul trips. Her only demand was that we would wake her up when there was food on offer!!!

We visited the Dominican Republic in the Caribbean where Lesley loved the laid-back attitudes and fun-loving spirits of the locals. We were all 'adopted' by a young, local waiter called Danny who would happily have come home with us at the end of our holiday - and the feeling was mutual. He would keep the best selection of cakes for us if we were late for the afternoon tea by the pool, delivering them personally to us on a napkin covered plate. I'm sure other people thought we were 'somebodies'.

Lesley's enjoyment and appreciation of good food also won us friends in Kitzbuhel where we stayed at the Hotel Tiefenbrunner for a second time after a mini-tour of Salzburg, Vienna, Budapest and Prague. Arriving at the hotel was like coming home and although it had been five years since our first stay there, restaurant staff remembered us immediately. Lesley would be offered extra desserts because she would enthusiastically say how much she had enjoyed whatever had been offered on the menu. There were also fresh pastries on offer each morning at breakfast which she loved. On our last morning we had to leave early and the pastries hadn't arrived – but the waiter ran out after us when we were getting on the coach for the airport with a bag for Lesley containing a selection of her favourites which had just been delivered. She was delighted – and so was the waiter. Restaurant staff simply became Lesley's friends over the course of a week or two and we often had a send-off from the staff of the hotels we stayed in mainly because they had enjoyed serving our appreciative, well-mannered daughter.

There were many holidays in Europe where we have been fortunate enough to visit most countries. A holiday to Cyprus was made more special than we had anticipated when I discovered on arrival that there was an option of a whole day in Egypt to visit Cairo and the Pyramids. I didn't expect Colin or Lesley to be up for it as it meant leaving our hotel at around 2.30 a.m. one day and not getting back for more than 24 hours – it was asking a lot. However, much to my surprise and delight, they were both enthusiastic and we booked the trip. It almost didn't go ahead because as we were crossing the tarmac to board the plane, people noticed what looked like a fuel leak and most of them refused to board the plane. I took the attitude that they would not have us flying if there was any danger and Colin and Lesley agreed, so along with a few others, we boarded and took our seats.

During the wait the stewardesses served us coffee and warm croissants which were delicious and most welcome after our early start. Time passed with the other people still out on the tarmac refusing to board and all I could think of was the packed itinerary ahead in Egypt which was being eaten into by the delay. I decided to ask if I could speak to the pilot and one of the stewardesses took me down to meet him. Thankfully his English was excellent and I asked him if there was any danger from the fuel leak. He explained that it had simply happened during refuelling and was of no concern at all, and that he would not put himself or his staff at risk at any time. I asked him if he would speak to the non-boarding passengers and tell them this as they weren't listening to the tour organisers – and perhaps he could say that they needed to get on immediately or choose to go back to the terminal building. Much to my surprise he agreed.

Within minutes some more people boarded while the rest got back on the coaches, opting out of the trip. We were soon underway with the other passengers who had boarded with us thanking me for my 'bottom-line Beth' attitude and for saving the trip. However, no one was more delighted than Lesley because, as a thank you from the staff, the three of us were served further fresh drinks and croissants and treated like royalty for the duration of the flight!

The day proved to be well worth the effort and although it was tiring, there was only one part that Lesley opted out of. We drove through Cairo and headed to Giza with the pyramids shimmering in the heat ahead of us as we travelled in our armed-guard staffed coach. More armed guards on foot or on camels awaited us at Giza which was a bit un-nerving but did not detract from the wonder of these 'Wonders of the World'. Entering the Great Pyramid was quite an effort for Lesley as it involved a steep, narrow, low-ceilinged descent into the foundations. We then had time in the coolness to marvel at the creations before climbing back out. Lesley was highly amused when Colin managed to worry the people passing us on their way downwards by asking them what day it was – and telling them that we had been down there since the previous Tuesday!!! I think a few just might have believed him at first. We then travelled to see the Great Sphinx which was truly amazing and we had time to relax and enjoy the Egyptian sunshine.

Following a wonderful buffet lunch overlooking the pyramids we headed back into the centre of Cairo for a museum visit which was probably more enthralling for Colin and me than it was for Lesley, but she tolerated it well, doing her very best to appear to be impressed by Tutankhamun though she passed on a close up view of unwrapped, mummified bodies! We then saw how papyrus was made and visited a jeweller's where we saw hieroglyphics being etched into gold ingots before heading to a river boat on the Nile. The comfortable river trip included an authentic evening meal with wonderful entertainment from belly-dancers and whirling dervishes while seeing views of Cairo from a different perspective. I think this was Lesley's favourite part of the day — chilling out in comfort with plenty of good food and drink.

By midnight we had headed to the souks which were still thronged with visitors, traders and beggars – and this was where Lesley decided that enough was enough, she was staying on the bus. I think Colin was delighted because he immediately said that he would be happy to stay with her – he never was a fan of markets at the best of times, and he too was shattered. Others from our wee party agreed but a few of us decided to make the effort and it was an amazing experience. Afterwards we headed back towards the airport and we were shocked by the number of cars and trucks on the busy roads who had no lights of any kind on their vehicles but who were hurtling along at high speed in the dark. We were most grateful to fall into our beds when we got back to the hotel in Cyprus but we all agreed that it had been a day of unrivalled experiences that we wouldn't have missed.

Not every day trip on holiday was as successful as that one. In Mexico I was very keen to visit the ancient Mayan city of Chichen Itza but it was quite a long way from our hotel. We booked to go on an organised excursion and enjoyed seeing a bit more of the Yucatan area on route. However, although Colin and I were very impressed with the ancient buildings, temples and square-based pyramids, Lesley was less than inspired and spent much of the time sitting in the shade of a tree looking rather miserable while we climbed the main pyramid. There wasn't even much on offer by way of food and drink to perk her up but we did manage to convince her to climb a bit of the way up the pyramid to get a photograph taken – which actually now makes it look as if she was perfectly happy to be there – as usual she had fixed her 'public face' in place! A sleep in the bus on the return journey had her back in good form in time for dinner at night though and she held no grudge about the long day.

For our thirtieth wedding anniversary we thought we would try something different with no real idea how any of us would feel about it. We booked a cruise and opted to go to the Baltic which proved to be a great choice. Lesley simply adored the whole cruising way of life. The days were structured and an evening newsletter would outline everything that was on offer the following day. Lesley would eagerly plan out the things she wanted to fit in around our trips ashore and she enjoyed such things as bean-bag bowls, line-dancing and West End style show-times. This was probably the best example of how much the prescriptive nature of the holiday suited her autistic needs. She could see all of her options and it was a simple task for us to sit down and plan activities to please us all and she was able to compromise on some of her choices because she knew that they would be offered again on other days. The entertainment staff got to know her well as she was keen to try out lots of their activities or to be an enthusiastic audience member for quizzes or karaoke sessions. We had a lovely cabin with a window and she enjoyed waking up to new views each day without the effort of packing and moving on.

Dressing for dinner at night after a busy day of sight-seeing and activities was the highlight as the food was superb and then simply having to walk to another area of the ship for live entertainment was the icing on the cake for our music-loving traveller. Lesley was obviously meant for the good things in life and she rose to the occasion daily. Colin and I fell in love with Tallinn on this trip but Lesley simply fell in love with cruising!

The following year we decided to plan another real adventure trip and this time Canada came to the fore. Initially we were simply intending visiting the attractions of the east of the country but I felt that if we were going to travel across the Atlantic anyway, we might as well try to fit in as much as we could. After a bit of research, I managed to come up with an amazing plan which would take us all the way to Vancouver by the end of the fortnight and we were all very excited.

Only one part of the trip was organised for us, the majority of it we had to do under our own steam, but Colin and Lesley had faith in my plans and arrangements. We arrived in Toronto and had to get a bus to Niagara for the first part of the adventure. Lesley loved Niagara Falls with the trip in the wee Maid of the Mist boat to be soaked by the spray from the falls being a real highlight.

Niagara was a bit commercialised but we had a lovely walk through the park the next day to see an amazing view of the falls cascading down with the power of the water even more apparent from the different perspective. The park was full of squirrels, some all red, some all black, some red with black tails and others black with red tails, very different to the common greys we were more used to at home.

We got a bus back to Toronto after another day and had a few days sight-seeing with the best bit for Lesley being dinner at the top of the CN Tower. The meal was excellent and the experience was reminiscent of the AMP Tower in Sydney but with the added bonus of being able to stand on a glass floor to look down to ground level and the baseball pitch next to the tower where they were preparing for an evening match. Colin decided that standing on the glass was a step too far, but Lesley was happy to take her lead from me – as usual!

The next step of the journey meant us making our way to the main railway station to get the train for Montreal early in the morning. I think Colin and I were both slightly nervous about the arrangements because I only had a slip with a booking number, no actual train tickets, though Lesley was completely sure that I had got it right – her trust in me was always unwavering. This was before we could rely on the internet to confirm things if necessary so we headed to the station with some trepidation. However, everything worked perfectly and we happily boarded the train and found seats two behind two, intending to keep swapping around so that no one was left alone for too long during the long journey.

We had just settled ourselves when we noticed a young couple with their baby boarding the carriage and they were struggling a bit to get themselves and their belongings on board. The young man had a form of dwarfism and his wife had a bad back malformation making walking difficult for her. We went forward to offer some assistance if they wanted it and they gratefully allowed us to get their belongings to the end of the carriage where there were seats on either side of the passageway with four seats facing each other. A notice announced that they were reserved for parties of three or four people but we assumed that they should have been booked in advance and returned to Lesley.

The young man, who had thanked us profusely, must then have noticed that we were a party of three and he came down to tell us that we could use the seats on the other side of the train from them, which meant we could enjoy the four-hour trip much more comfortably, with no one left on their own at all.

The couple were good company and we soon learned that the young Canadian man had been volunteering in Vietnam where he met the girl who was to become his wife. Having married in Vietnam and had their baby the following year, they were on their first visit together to his parents near Montreal and there was great excitement to be introducing them to their grandson. We were full of admiration for the spirit that took this young man so far away from home to volunteer in spite of his own limitations and we realised that any physical difficulties were more than compensated for by his intelligence, personality and humour. Just as we were of our daughter, I'm sure his parents were extremely proud of him and his achievements.

By the time we settled for a few days in Montreal I was very glad that this was not the end of the holiday as one big, built-up city tends to look quite like the previous one. We were well treated in our hotel when we showed we were willing to try to use our French and we were treated to a continental breakfast each morning with the best croissants in the world – according to Lesley who knew what she was talking about. We had a meal one night in the Pickle Barrel Restaurant and as usual, after the main course, we asked Lesley if she was having a pudding. Also as usual, she initially said that she wasn't going to until we encouraged her a little and she would say 'Oh all right then!' as if she was doing us a big favour. Well that night she really was. We simply ordered coffees and she chose an ice cream sundae from a picture on the menu. The waitress arrived carrying what appeared to be a glass display container and three long spoons – and we then realised that this huge monstrosity of various fruits, ice creams, sauces and toppings was the one portion dessert that Lesley had ordered. It had sparklers, umbrellas, cherries, you name it – if anything could be added to an ice cream, it had been thought of here – hence the three spoons. None of us could eat for laughing but I have to say, we did make a huge effort and polished it off much to the amusement of our waitress and we left the restaurant with Lesley highly satisfied with her evening out.

A day trip to Quebec was the best part of our Montreal stay and we all loved the quaint, old-worldly feel of the city which had wonderful wall murals and trompe l'oeil art work on gable ends of buildings. The French influence was strong as was the Native Canadian feel with dream-catchers everywhere. If Quebec had been closer to home I'm sure we would have returned for a longer stay. However again it was time to move on.

The next step of the journey involved us making our way to Montreal airport for the flight to Calgary and we were glad to find that all my arrangements were spot on and we were soon flying over miles and miles of nothing more than salt-pans. It was amazing to spend so long in a plane in daylight hours without seeing anything much in the way of habitation below us, but Lesley managed to sleep her way across country to arrive refreshed in Calgary. We had time to explore Calgary on our two-night stopover and discovered that the famous Calgary Stampede had just finished with the remnants of hay bales greeting us all over the town.

The organised part of our holiday started when we boarded a coach to take us through the Rockies to Banff, Lake Louise, Lac Le Jeune and on to Vancouver. This was where the holiday really started with the most amazing scenery all around us every day. Just when you thought you couldn't see anything better, there was an even better view around the next corner and we were treated to some amazing wildlife too. Bears, moose, bald eagles, ospreys and mountain goats abounded and our coach driver was a wonderful lady who was happy to pull over to let us enjoy anything of interest. Lesley was able to relax in the coach with there being just a very small group of us, and we got to know each other quickly through our shared enjoyment of our surroundings. Once again I think people were amazed by our daughter's ability to take it all in her stride and simply have cat-naps in the bus when she was feeling a bit tired. She was really proving to be the most admirable of world travellers and we were proud of her achievements and her efforts to cope with all the experiences on offer.

She went on to enjoy helping me to tempt wild marmosets and macaws out of the trees with bits of banana in Brazil during another holiday. We had made the trip there to allow Colin to fulfil his dream of visiting the Maracanã Stadium in Rio but although Lesley enjoyed the trip up the Corcovado, the best bit of this holiday for her was when we moved up the coast for a more relaxing second week. She loved the friendliness of the hotel waiters and waitresses who came for hilarious English lessons every morning at breakfast time from Colin whose grasp of Portuguese greatly impressed them. Lesley loved all the resulting banter and again they just took her to their hearts.

The following year we took on a trip to South Africa with part of our tour to include a two-day safari, which we weren't sure Lesley would particularly enjoy. How wrong could we have been?

She enjoyed staying in Cape Town at first and coped better than us when our luggage was missing for four days! She also enjoyed our tour of the Garden Route especially when we went to visit an elephant sanctuary where she again fell in love, this time with Nandy and Tandy, a mother and child pair who loved having her feed them and stroke them. She was absolutely mesmerised by their gentleness in spite of their size and would have stayed there for hours quite happily. When we came home she was thrilled when I got her a t-shirt printed with one of the photographs of her favourite duo – it was a real treasure in her collection of t-shirts from around the world.

The best bit of the holiday for all of was the visit to Aquila for our safari. The weather had dropped below freezing – we were there during the South African winter – and we had to go out at dusk and then again at dawn to have the best chance of seeing the animals. An icy wind was blowing as we climbed aboard the jeep on the first night and we set off feeling very excited in a party totalling just us and four others. We were amazed by the number of different animals we saw by the time the skies had darkened and even then we were still able to pick out the eyes of the lions on the hills just above us. Our driver was a real character and at one point he pretended that the jeep had broken down – when in actual fact he was about to offer us a glass of champagne as the sun went down. Lesley was even more impressed when he produced a flask of hot chocolate and asked if anyone would prefer that to the champagne and we stood together wrapped in blankets, toasting the wonderful South African wildlife.

On arriving back at our base, we were told that the morning trip would leave before 6.00 a.m. with breakfast not being served until the tour was over. We were also warned that the overnight forecast was for the weather to get even colder and wetter. After our wonderful dinner, we were guided by torch down to our huts where a log fire had been lit and where the beds were draped in magnificent, thick fleece blankets. We told Lesley that she could simply stay in bed in the morning and we would come for her after the safari to go for breakfast – but she was utterly shocked by our suggestion. She said she had loved every minute of the day and she wouldn't miss any of it no matter how early the start or how bad the weather. We were so proud of her and very glad that we were again going to share the experience as 'The Three Musketeers'.

Next morning, one couple had dropped out so it was just us and two young South African brothers who headed out for the next part of the adventure. The storm during the night had unsettled some of the animals and we had to make a quick reverse to avoid some angry buffalo followed by an even quicker retreat when a couple of feuding elephants turned on our jeep. However, we also had lions padding along just a yard away from us and the wonderful experience of watching giraffes glide past us with their beautiful, flowing movement while we sat watching rhinos, zebras and all varieties of antelopes. Lesley loved every minute of it and had certainly earned the delicious breakfast that awaited us when we returned – though Timothy, our driver, had again provided coffee and hot chocolate part-way through the trip.

As we ate, we could hear beautiful singing coming from the kitchen and we asked if it was a radio playing. When we were told that it was the staff singing while they worked, we asked for them to be told that they were making a wonderful sound and that we appreciated being able to hear it. A few minutes later, five members of staff came out, stood at our table and sang unaccompanied in perfect five-part harmony – just because we had shown our appreciation. We were truly humbled and they were just delighted that they had given us pleasure. I sometimes think that we do appreciate things more than most people because of our journey through life with Lesley and she herself was always someone who was grateful for the little things as much as the big things.

Every Day Life

It was good to be at a stage where we knew that Lesley had decided that there would be no further operations and we just had to deal with day to day life rather than having bigger worries looming ahead. This didn't necessarily mean that life had become 'easy' but then, is it ever for anyone? One of the most difficult issues to deal with was my Dad having developed Alzheimer's, deteriorating very quickly into a world where we couldn't really reach him. Lesley found it very hard at first to cope with the loss of the Papa she had always had such a bond with and would worry about not knowing what to say or how to react when his behaviour was really strange. However, throughout all the years of his decline from home to hospital and then to nursing home, she visited a couple of times every week and loved him till the day he died. She also appreciated how difficult it was for her Nana as she was aware of what a devoted couple they had always been and how they had shared everything in life until the illness intervened. Her Nana visited her Papa every day and as well as the visits to see her Papa, Lesley had dinner every Monday night with her Nana too because she thought that was only fair. She was always the most loyal and caring of people who hated to think that she was making more of one person than another.

Her other loyalty every week was visiting her friend Leigh in Whitburn. Leigh's health sometimes wasn't too good and Lesley hated to think of her being unable to get out and about and not getting many visitors, so as Friday was her day off work, it became their day together. Sometimes they would simply have a chat, watch television and have a snack lunch. Other times they would make the trip to Livingston and have lunch out together. With Leigh's general health seeming to have improved at one point, I raised the possibility of them going away together for a long weekend. I wasn't sure how they would cope or how Leigh would react to the suggestion but felt it was something that they could take on if it was a well organised trip. They both jumped at the idea and after some consideration, Blackpool was the first choice.

I took them to their pick-up point for the coach and dropped Leigh's wee cat off at the cattery and then worried that if it didn't work out, I would be to blame for suggesting it in the first place. I needn't have been concerned as they had a ball and came back asking me to help them to choose a similar trip to a different place for the following year. They went on to have a further two trips away which again they both enjoyed and they handled little problems well together. It was great to hear that Lesley was happy to speak up for herself on these trips and become a bit more self-confident. One hotel only had marmalade out for the toast in the morning but as Lesley didn't like marmalade, she asked a waitress if there was any jam, and was given some immediately. Another time they didn't like the evening entertainment and decided just to watch television in their room. Leigh didn't think they would be allowed to take a drink up to their room and would need to stay in the lounge if they wanted anything. Lesley told her that it would be all right because we would do that on holiday as a family but Leigh still didn't feel it was right – so Lesley asked the bartender who happily obliged and they enjoyed the rest of their evening relaxing in the room with their J2Os. This might not seem like much, but it was major for us and we were very optimistic about the growing confidence that it showed Lesley was developing.

The wee holidays meant Lesley was now saving up for another aspect of her life and budgeting was quite an issue for her. She had a savings box with various compartments and she used this to plan for her daily, weekly and annual expenditure. Usually it worked very well but there was one year when it caught her out big time – and I should have seen it coming. Lesley's love of music meant that her one luxury in life was buying CDs and any extra money she had left over from her day to day expenses would be used to purchase the latest CD on her list. One year she appeared to be managing to buy more than the usual amount and I commented on how she was affording the extra ones. She would happily say that she had money in her 'extras' the compartment where she put any left-over money from her weekly outgoings or from her 'entertainment' section if she hadn't been out much. She saved every week towards Christmas and birthday presents, holidays and for her football and speedway season tickets too.

In October or November each year, when the speedway season had finished, current season ticket holders were always given the opportunity to buy the following year's ticket in advance for a reduced price and we always took advantage of the offer. When the letter arrived I told Lesley how much she needed to give me for her season ticket so that I could then write a cheque for all three of us, which was our usual procedure. Lesley immediately went to her room to count out her money but after some time had passed she returned to the living room looking very sheepish and asked if I would come to help her to count the notes.

The notes were lying beside her computer and I began to count them, only to find that she was well short of what she needed. I asked her where the rest of the money was and she got rather upset – and then the whole story came out. Lesley had moved the money into an envelope because the compartment in her savings box was full. She had never been good with numbers or values and she had genuinely thought that she had 'over-saved' for football and speedway because it had looked like a lot of money. She had decided to move some of it to her 'extras' section and had then used it to buy CDs. She was horrified when I told her that not only did she not have enough for her speedway ticket, if she gave me what she had, she would have nothing for football tickets either – and she had the whole winter ahead with her and her Dad intending to go to selected games. Dismay reigned!

It would of course have been easy – and kind – for me to simply bale her out, pay her speedway ticket and help her with the football. However due to her lack of awareness with the value of things, I felt that this would not help her to develop more financial awareness, something that would be more important for her in the future if she didn't have me helping her to plan and budget. So, much to Colin's horror, I took a hard line.

I explained how long it would take for her to save the balance due and then told her that the season ticket would by then be considerably more expensive. Meanwhile she would have no money to go to football matches if she was focussing on speedway. I asked her to think it through and tell me what she thought would work. It was always horrible to see Lesley upset and that night she was really berating herself for being, in her words, an idiot, so I quickly returned to her room to stop her getting too distraught. She was delighted when I said that the best thing might be for me to pay the ticket and for her to pay me back weekly as much as she could – without having to miss out on any football matches with her Dad.

Her relief and gratitude were overwhelming – you would have thought I had given her thousands of pounds rather than just under a hundred. She immediately went to her computer and made a little chart showing how much she owed me with boxes to allow her to write in what she had paid back. I was very proud of her attitude and even more proud that nothing like this ever happened again – a lesson learned the hard way, but learned well. When the deposit for the next wee holiday with Leigh was due, she gave it to me from her savings and then again used a chart so that she could pay money to me weekly to save for the balance and keep a record herself of what she owed. This worked for her as she could keep changing the balance to be aware of how much she still had to pay and after that she could focus on saving for holiday spending.

Things didn't always come easily to Lesley but we were so proud of how hard she worked in all areas of her life to be the best she could be – and she loved to get a bit of praise when we felt that she had come up with a good system for dealing with the more difficult concepts.

During these years when Lesley was in her twenties, there was quite a lot of balance and routine in our lives which helped Lesley to cope. We all went to work, Lesley had the various weekly things that she did and we had learned to try to keep everything as calm as possible for her by planning and structuring the things we did as a family and made great efforts not to change anything at the last minute. Sadly, even with her daily medication, this couldn't always prevent the build-up of emotions that would result in the eruption of real rages in the house but things had been a lot better and Lesley was much happier with life in general. However, she had been getting more easily tired and was often rather pale and I put most of this down to the heavy periods that plagued her life every month and which she hated trying to cope with.

One day we were heading for home in the car and I was suddenly aware that she had stopped talking and had slowly lifted her right arm and was staring at her hand. I asked her if there was a problem and she didn't answer and I then became aware of her breathing being a bit strange with a sort of clicking noise deep in her throat. Again I asked if she was all right and this time she turned and looked at me quite blankly and I was struck by the paleness of her skin so as soon as I could, I pulled off the road.

I held her hand and within a minute or so she lost the blank expression and was able to tell me that she had suddenly felt very strange and that her hand had tingled and felt clammy but that she was feeling all right. When we arrived home minutes later she fell asleep on the couch, still looking very pale though she appeared to be fine when she woke up. The next night she was sitting watching television when another similar episode happened, again starting with the very slow raising of her hand and continuing in almost exactly the same way as the day before. I was a bit concerned particularly by the blankness in Lesley's eyes and her pale complexion and strange breathing.

When she had recovered I had a wee chat with her and explained that she seemed to have gone into her 'own wee world' for a couple of minutes. She was aware of the same feelings in her hand but hadn't been aware of me then holding her hand until she 'came around' fully. I told her that it might be wise to make sure that she sat down somewhere safe if she got the strange feelings in her hand again, just in case she fell and hurt herself and I also told her to let me know if it happened again when I wasn't there. Lesley accepted my calm attitude as proof that she didn't need to worry about it but did have to be aware and she said it was probably just because she was a bit tired.

For a few weeks there was nothing else but then she came home one day and said that it had happened at her work – and then there were another three episodes within a couple of days. I decided to write down the dates of all of the little attacks and said that if it happened again we should speak to a doctor about it. A few weeks later there was another cluster of the 'wee daft turns' as Lesley referred to them and we made an appointment to see a GP. I wasn't sure if there was any link with her general tiredness and heavy periods but I also felt that they might be little 'petit mal' episodes which I had seen in children in my teaching career.

Lesley wanted to see a female doctor if we were going to talk about period issues and she said that there was a doctor that her friend always went to see because she was very caring, so we made the appointment with her. It turned out to be a good choice because Dr Brown listened carefully to everything we had to say about Lesley's health in general and the recent attacks in particular. She said that she thought it would be a good idea to have blood tests done as a matter of course but that it might also be wise to refer Lesley to a specialist to discuss the little 'absences' that had been happening.

We were asked to go back to see her when the blood test result came back and this was because it had shown that Lesley had very low iron levels and a very low platelet count. Dr Brown asked if Lesley was bleeding excessively if she got any cuts but since that hadn't happened at all in recent times, it was of no help. The very heavy periods were the only other indication of anything related to blood loss – and the tiredness that we had already discussed. It was quite simple to prescribe tablets to improve the iron levels but the doctor didn't want to automatically start Lesley on steroids for the low platelets unless this proved to be the only option. She got advice from a consultant and it was agreed that if the count reached 100 and could be maintained there, then Lesley could just be monitored regularly and her iron levels boosted as required.

This became just a routine six-monthly check which worked well and the steroids were not required though the levels remained quite low. The monthly problems did not improve and this had to be dealt with further down the line. The more important issue at this point was a referral to meet Dr Duncan at the Western General in Edinburgh to investigate the little episodes which continued to occur in small clusters every few weeks. We made the trip in to the city with Lesley showing quite a bit of apprehension and I had to reassure her all we needed to do was talk to the doctor and get her advice. Again we were fortunate to meet a doctor who was down to earth, open, honest and who listened. Lesley told her that she would prefer it if I answered the questions because she got a bit muddled when she was nervous and Dr Duncan was happy to agree to this but she continued to give Lesley her place by checking everything with her too.

She asked a lot about the early years and the surgery that had taken place then as well as the issues of the imbalance left in the first few years after the major surgery which had resulted temporarily in a type of epilepsy. Her plan was to arrange brain scans and heart tests to give her a better picture of what might be going on and the arrangements were made that day to have some of the tests done immediately and then later to have a heart monitor fitted to do 24 hour tracings. Lesley was reassured by the doctor's calm manner and we duly went off to begin the tests.

The brain scan was also arranged and Lesley was a bit concerned because she couldn't remember the last time she had gone through similar procedures. I reminded her of the time when, as a baby, she had a scan done while I fed her with a bottle of milk – she hadn't even noticed the scan because it didn't cause her any problems and she just enjoyed her bottle. We had a laugh about this and it stopped her worrying. In fact, when she came out after it had all been completed, she said she had been so relaxed that she had nodded off to sleep.

The doctor had told us that she would write to us when she had all of the results but she had already confirmed that Lesley was having small seizures and gave Lesley options on how to move on. We could wait to see how things progressed, doing nothing for as long as Lesley felt that the symptoms were bearable and only reacting further if the episodes got worse. The other option was to begin to take medication right away. I was already recording the dates and frequencies of the attacks and could continue to do this so that we would notice any escalation and if Lesley was losing consciousness, then that would indicate treatment was necessary.

Lesley and I talked about it and she was happier to leave things as they were, telling the doctor that she always had time to make sure she was sitting down and that the only annoying thing was feeling the need to sleep afterwards. When the full results came in, they were a bit concerning though Lesley took it that because she didn't need to take any tablets, everything must be fine. It was difficult to tell whether some aspects of damage and shrinkage showing in the brain were as a result of all the early interventions or if there was current deterioration taking place. Colin and I played it down with Lesley and said that obviously all of her big operations would have caused some damage but we were really worried and wondered how things were going to progress. Dr Duncan was willing, with Lesley's permission, to speak to me on the phone about the results and we were reassured that further investigations would take place when required. Thankfully, the little absences didn't get any worse and we knew that we could go straight back to Dr Duncan if we were worried.

In spite of health concerns, life was always as normal as we could make it and we continued to enjoy all our good times and live life with lots of humour and with lots of love. Holidays continued to be an important part of Lesley's life and she always loved to have one planned and booked. We decided that we fancied somewhere else far afield and different. Peru was discussed as I had always wanted to see Machu Picchu but on further investigation I was left feeling rather worried about the effects of travelling at high altitude. We thought that it was a risk not worth taking in case it was particularly difficult for Lesley so we opted for China instead.

This proved to be an amazing holiday but one that came with some trials due to the effects of the Icelandic ash cloud on air travel. To put it simply, we got stuck in Beijing for an extra week. We had been privileged to see the temples and palaces of the capital, the Terracotta Warriors of Xian and the Great Wall at Jinshanling. Initially the extended stay gave us a couple of free days which allowed us to explore Beijing on our own and we made the best of the opportunity by exploring using the wonderful underground. We visited the Olympic Stadium and tracked down the football stadium where the strip turned out to be very similar to that of Hibs. We also ate in a little, local restaurant at night and shopped in a local supermarket giving us a chance to mix with Chinese people in a non-touristy manner. It was a great experience though the following days proved to be more difficult. We had to check out of the hotel at 7.00 a.m. each day and travel miles to the airport on the off-chance of there being a flight – only to return to the hotel by evening.

This was very hard for Lesley due to the uncertainty of what was going to happen and the fact that we should all have been back at work. We were fortunate that we could still stay in the hotel and have the rooms paid for but we had to check in to a different room each day and again this was particularly stressful for Lesley. Yet she remained as strong and calm as she could and I only remember one day when she got rather tearful and needed the reassurance that the Three Musketeers were in it together and that we would not allow ourselves to be spilt up if only one or two seats were ever offered. The rest of the people in our small group stayed together and the numbers going to eat in the little restaurant grew each night when we told them of the very cheap food and wonderful service. We were treated like royalty and the language problem was no barrier to the mutual respect and friendship that developed.

By the end of the week, and on another day when we had been waiting around for hours, there was suddenly great excitement when we were offered enough seats on a flight to London for all but two of our group. A lovely couple who had become our closest compatriots during the difficult days were asked to wait for the next flight and we felt so sorry to be leaving them behind in spite of our great relief to be on the way home. Fortunately, they were able to be slotted on to the next flight so hadn't been left alone for too long. We had huge admiration for the strength of character Lesley displayed during this difficult time and indeed she showed up some other more selfish travellers who could only think of themselves.

The experience didn't put us off travelling and we followed China with a trip to Borneo, which in all honesty was mainly because of my love of orang utans, but which turned out to be Lesley's spiritual home. She adored everything about the holiday – the hotel, the food, the weather, the wildlife and more importantly, the people. She loved their gentleness, their beautiful smiles and the respect and consideration they showed everyone. One waitress, Zalipa, became extremely fond of Lesley and they looked forward to seeing each other every day. It turned out that her husband had some disabilities and she just so admired Lesley for being the lovely person she was and for the way she thanked everyone so sincerely for anything they did for her. On our last night Zalipa had organised a special farewell meal for us with a beautifully prepared table with fresh flowers and special tableware, the hotel musicians coming to play for us and our drinks being 'on the house'. She had flowers for me and a lovely bracelet for Lesley and it was an incredibly emotional night for everyone. We were thanked by the management for treating their staff so well and for being a pleasure to serve – but in reality it was Lesley who was being honoured and Colin and I were so touched by these wonderful people. None of us will ever forget a moment of that holiday and Lesley didn't need to pause for thought if anyone asked her after that to choose her favourite holiday – Borneo won hands down.

Future Plans

Special holidays like that one helped to make up for the hard times and I think we valued them more than most people. The Borneo holiday almost hadn't happened due to Colin and I being 'run over' by a driver who came through a red light on a 'green man' crossing and breaking our toes the week before we were due to go. The major factor in this episode was that we realised how close we had come to Lesley having perhaps lost both of us in one accident and I realised that no one in 'officialdom' would have had any idea of how needy our daughter was and the help and support that she would need if she didn't have us. It was a wake-up call and I knew that I had to take action to ensure that Lesley was not ever left in such a vulnerable position.

We had always coped with all of Lesley's needs on our own, but this meant that there was no outside support in place or knowledge of the difficulties Lesley faced in daily life. She wanted to continue to live with us and we had always said that when only one of us was left, that parent would then need to make arrangements for Lesley's future. The accident changed my views on this and I began the process of getting Lesley 'known'. It was very difficult because Lesley needed to be involved in the process but she didn't want any of it to happen. We reassured her, to the best of our ability that nothing was going to change in the short-term but that we did have to be sure that her needs would be met when she no longer had us to rely on and I think she understood the necessity even though disapproving of the actions.

We contacted a specialist lawyer so that we could make our wills more relevant and fit for purpose. We went through the process of setting up a trust fund for Lesley that would kick in when she was on her own and would be managed to provide for all of her needs. We also took out Powers of Attorney and Colin and I wrote 'living wills' that made clear our wishes that should we lose our mental faculties we would not be medicated if medical conditions were causing physical deterioration. We could think of nothing worse for Lesley than being left with a parent who was helpless and who didn't know her and could not be capable of giving her the love and care that she needed.

With all of this done I also contacted the social work department and we were allocated a social worker who was shocked that a young lady in her thirties with Lesley's needs was being offered no support. We explained that it was more a case of making sure that Lesley was 'in the system' so that when she needed care, it would be simpler to have that put in place. There followed a lot of assessments and meetings to ensure that the whole picture was as clear as possible and some of it was very hard for Lesley to cope with though she got to know and trust her social worker and was eventually able to have a laugh with her. We were asked about respite care for Lesley for the first time and initially I just said that this was not something that we had ever been offered or considered. On reflection I wondered if it would be a way of Lesley beginning to experience the challenges of little snippets of life without me on hand so Colin and I discussed it fully. We then talked to Lesley about finding out more and though she was reluctant, she agreed to give it a try.

Further meetings were required to determine where Lesley should go. Her combination of problems made it difficult to be sure which provision was most appropriate for her due to there being respite provision for people with physical needs and separate ones for those with learning needs. Lesley was a combination of both and she needed to have IQ tests to determine which facility would be best for her. The physical needs were made the priority and we met with members of staff from Cornerstone which was only a twenty minute drive away from us.

After much preparation, Lesley was invited for her first visit, an overnight stay with me taking her on the Saturday afternoon and due to collect her again on the Sunday morning. She was very nervous, understandably, but I was being matter of fact about it all and giving her no chance of backing out. We spoke to her on the phone that night and were aware that she didn't seem very happy but we just tried to act as though there was nothing wrong and said it would soon be the next morning. When I collected her she thanked the staff and smiled and appeared to be all right – but as soon as we went out to the car she erupted and said it had been awful and she would never go back. I had to work hard at not over-reacting and just gave her a big hug and said we would discuss it when we got home. She sat in silence on the return journey and then once in her own house, her rage grew. We had a lot of door-banging and storming about the house but she couldn't tell us exactly what had happened.

It was not until late that night that I managed to get her calm enough to talk about her experience and then I realised that she was justified in feeling angry. Lesley would never have made a fuss or asked for anything but this had led to her being left completely on her own. After she had eaten her evening meal she had been told that she could sit in the big, open lounge area to watch television and that someone would be along to keep her company. However, this did not happen. A couple of times she was asked, in the passing, if there was anything she needed and of course she just said no. This meant that she didn't even get anything to drink and she was too shy to ask. She would have preferred to have been sitting in her own bedroom where there also was a television but she didn't want to leave the lounge as she still believed that someone would be coming.

I was now feeling very angry as this was not the scene that had been painted to us before she went and I felt that Lesley had been let down. A lot of money was being paid for this respite and although Lesley only had to contribute a small amount, her needs had not been met in the way that had been outlined. I told Lesley that I would speak to the social worker about what had happened and let her know that Lesley would not be returning but before I could do this the next day I had a phone call from the depute manager to talk about Lesley's visit. She thought from the reports that had been left that Lesley had enjoyed her stay and was looking forward to returning and she was shocked when I said that Lesley had hated every minute and would not be going back. She asked me to tell her what had gone wrong and was very upset when I outlined the fact that nothing had happened which was the real problem. The members of staff who had been on duty had just said that Lesley was no problem at all and that it would be great to have her back but they had obviously misinterpreted the situation and had simply thought that there was no effort involved in meeting Lesley's needs.

We were asked to attend a meeting with the social worker present and the management team and Lesley received an apology for what she had experienced during her stay. They wanted her to go back to give them another chance and assured her that it would be completely different next time. Reluctantly, Lesley agreed and I am thankful that she was brave enough to do this when I know she really didn't want to. We decided that she would try two nights the next time so that she had more of a chance to get to know people and with the understanding that if things were no better, I would collect her earlier. This time she was allocated a named member of staff who was to be there for at least some of the time on both days and who would make sure that Lesley was happier. Having discussed what Lesley liked to do, they made a trip in the bus to the shops in Livingston and had lunch out together. On a one to one basis Lesley was always more able to chat and this allowed her to show that she had a sense of fun and a great sense of humour and a good relationship quickly developed. Saturday night was a take-away meal treat and Lesley was able to choose her favourite Chicken Korma. At other times there was lots of chatting and Lesley enjoyed helping in the kitchen.

When I collected her this time – with some trepidation in spite of her having sounded cheery on the phone – she was beaming and giving hugs before we left. She had already been discussing when she might be back next and what they might do and I knew that it was real and not just her good manners kicking in. On the way home I heard all about it in great detail and then everything was repeated for her Dad's benefit. By the end of the next visit a couple of months later, she was talking about it being her 'home from home' and she was obviously well-liked by the staff. She had two or three days every other month and got to know the set-up, the staff and some of the residents. She would go out to the shops, to cafes or ten-pin bowling near-by. It became obvious that she was comfortable in the environment and she began to say when she needed help to wash her hair or deal with any other problems, though this remained difficult for her.

As well as helping Lesley to move on, Colin and I enjoyed a relaxing couple of days each time. We went out for a meal a couple of times but mostly just enjoyed having lazy mornings –

Lesley hated it if we sat around having a relaxing breakfast still in our dressing gowns at the weekend so we felt quite wicked if we did this, like two naughty children given a free rein. We were all happy that the right place had been found and the social worker monitored the progress and was delighted with the eventual success.

At this time, we had also decided that a formal diagnosis of autism might be helpful in meeting Lesley's needs in the future and I asked for a referral. Initially, Dr Kerr, the GP, was reluctant and felt no need to look for an additional label for Lesley but I told him that we had to think of the future when I wasn't around to ensure Lesley got the help she needed. The Apert's Syndrome label would not tell people of Lesley's social, emotional and behavioural difficulties in the way that Autism Spectrum Disorder would and he admitted that he had not thought of it in this way and was then more than willing to organise a prompt referral. It only took one afternoon visit from a specialist who came out from Edinburgh to make the formal diagnosis and Lesley was reassured that this would make no difference to her day to day life but might be of huge benefit in the future. This had all taken a year of hard work and emotional turmoil but we felt happy that we were better set up to ensure the best possible life for Lesley when she no longer had her parents for support.

The diagnosis also led to the social worker saying that Lesley could have a place with Autism Initiatives which might help her to come to terms with her difficulties and she agreed to try this too.

Cooking was identified as being an activity that could be the starting point for her and Tuesday afternoons were organised. She would finish work a little bit early and go straight to A.I. where she would spend a couple of hours cooking, chatting and getting to know other people. It worked to an extent and there were members of staff she really liked and enjoyed talking to. However, after a number of months she told me that she found it all too tiring and that she didn't feel she was getting much out of it. I asked her to stick with it for a bit longer to see if things improved for her and we had a chat with one of the senior workers about a couple of issues that had arisen and he tried to address the problems. After a few more weeks though she told me that it was just becoming too much, that she was dreading a Tuesday and I agreed that we could just focus on her doing more cooking at home and continue with her occasional respite stays. She was sorry to say goodbye but felt she was doing the right thing and I had to respect her for being able to talk it through with us and come to her own decision. I think she was growing in confidence and beginning to value herself a bit more which really pleased her Dad and me.

Due to my early breast cancer, Lesley was at high risk and had to start being carefully monitored by the time she was into her thirties. This just added another level of hospital rounds that she accepted as being a necessary part of her life. She had previously had a lump which was fully investigated and found to be of no concern but after the formal monitoring started we had another real scare. A worrying physical examination led to tests where changes showed up and scans and needle biopsies were taken to check further. We received a frightening letter that the biopsy had shown tissue changes which were cause for concern and which meant that further investigation was required. We had an immediate appointment to go back in to see the doctor for further investigation. He explained that he was worried about the changes that had shown up in the mammograms, scans and needle biopsy following his physical examination and he now wanted to perform punch biopsies of both breasts. Not having undergone this procedure myself I wasn't too sure of what was involved but Lesley said that she was happy to go through with it as long as her Mum could stay and hold her hand. The doctor said that it wasn't a very pleasant thing to see either but Lesley and I were a great team when things were tough and this proved to be the case again.

She was calm and remained relaxed while various areas on both sides were sampled so that all of the tissue could be thoroughly checked. Lesley didn't complain at all when it was all over and even wondered if she should go back to her work for the afternoon! I think she was relieved when I said that going home for a rest might be a better idea but again her courage and fortitude would be an example to most people and it was with great pride that I told her Dad about the events of the day and the courage she had shown. The really good news came with the results as the changes were not malignancies and Lesley would just continue to require careful monitoring each year. I remember once being told that when Mother Nature goes wrong she goes wrong with a vengeance and this so often seemed to be true for Lesley – but thankfully at least this time Mother Nature seemed to have been stopped in her tracks.

Lesley did not dwell on things once they were past and she went on with making the most of all the things she enjoyed. Her general aches and pains tended to be getting worse as was her tiredness but she coped admirably and nothing stopped her from going to her voluntary work every day, visiting her Nana and Papa, going out with her friends and continuing to support Hibernian football club and Edinburgh Monarchs speedway team. Her resilience was tested greatly by the death of her beloved Papa and although he had been very ill for so long she felt the loss deeply. The funeral was a very difficult day for her but again she managed to be brave and strong and coped with a dignity that her Papa would have been proud of. She continued to have her Monday night meal every week with her Nana knowing how much of a loss she had sustained and Lesley tried so hard to empathise.

Just before her Papa died there had been a fundraising Bingo night at the Nursing Home and Lesley had won a beautiful big cuddly dog toy. Without even pausing for thought when she collected her prize she declared that she wanted her Papa to have it in his room. I told her that he wouldn't be aware of it but she was adamant that she wanted to take it up to his room before we left that night. Her Papa might not have been able to admire it but the carers and nurses all loved it and made sure that it sat on his bed and got moved into the best position every time her Papa was turned.

After his death my Mum asked if I thought Lesley would like to have 'Papa's Pooch' returned to her and I said I would ask her. I wasn't sure how she would feel about this but she was overjoyed and the cuddly dog sat on her bed every day thereafter. For a while, when she was feeling very sad about the loss of her Papa, the dog would be brought through to the living room and she would sit cuddling it for hours. Eventually this need became less as her acceptance of the loss became easier to bear but now and again we would know how she was feeling if Pooch made an appearance and it became a bit of a yardstick for us to gauge Lesley's emotional fragility.

Happy occasions were always built in to our lives as much as possible to counter-act the hard times. One such occasion early in 2012 gave Lesley one of the best trips of her life. There had been a local radio competition with the prize being a trip to London for two with a champagne afternoon tea with Jason Donovan. I heard in the car that it was the final day to enter and checked with Lesley that she had remembered about it – and she hadn't, so late that night she went online and left her name. On the Friday we were taking Leigh home with her and Lesley chatting in the car when I heard mention of the competition winners – and to our shock, the name Lesley McRobb was mentioned! I was screaming with joy for her and we eagerly waited to hear more with Lesley checking that I would go with her if she had indeed won. It would have been lovely to have sent her off with a friend but she didn't feel that she would cope with any of it unless I was with her. Lesley got a phone call later on which she then asked me to deal with because she was scared she would miss something vital.

We were to be given return rail tickets to London with an overnight in a hotel and the afternoon tea in a 'posh' hotel. We were buzzing with excitement as it was only a week away – thankfully we were free to go. I spoke to Colin and we decided that since we were going to London anyway – and it was many years since we had been to the capital – we should make the most of it and cram in as much as possible. I managed to get tickets for 'The Lion King' for the evening after the afternoon tea and Lesley asked if there would be any chance of a trip on the London Eye which was easily arranged.

Things went like clockwork. Colin took us to the station and we enjoyed our trip down. We found our hotel and then headed out to meet Jason in a lovely hotel not far from Buckingham Palace. While we were waiting in reception, Billy Connolly came in with armloads of designer shopping bags and Lesley asked him for his autograph which he delightedly gave her while he enjoyed his audience with a 'fan' and had a good blether with her. A young waiter grinned after Billy left and told Lesley that she had got 'two for the price of one' that day, seeing Billy before Jason.

I can't stress how lovely Jason Donovan was. There were just a few tables of invited guests and he made his way around each of them, finishing with us. The other couple at our table had told us that they just liked to enter competitions rather than being fans of Jason and when he settled himself down beside us and got champagne and tea to have with us, it was really Lesley who became the star of the show. He was delighted to hear that she had first loved him in Neighbours, had met him at the SECC many years previously, had been to see him performing in Joseph and had voted for him every week when he was in 'Strictly Come Dancing'. He happily posed for photographs and gave his autograph and signed his new CD – adding 'especially for you' and 'thanks for all your votes on 'Strictly'. Lesley was in seventh heaven. We walked down to Buckingham Palace afterwards and the show went well that night but Lesley was exhausted after such a long day. I was delighted to see little pedalled rickshaws outside the theatre at the end of the show and I gratefully hired one to take us back to the underground. It was a chilly March evening and the driver wrapped us up in a fleece blanket much to the delight of my sleepy daughter.

Next morning, we went on the London Eye first thing, which Lesley loved, and then we took a Thames river boat to see the sights without Lesley having to do any more walking. A quick lunch on the embankment followed before we headed back to get our luggage. I have to mention that, as a huge Chelsea fan myself, I noticed we would be passing by the tube stop for Chelsea's football stadium and I suggested that we could maybe get off just to let me see the outside of the ground. When I later told Colin about Lesley's response to my suggestion he almost choked! 'On your bike, Mum, this is my trip and I'm shattered!!!' My generous-hearted daughter who would do anything for anyone had her limits - and had just reached them! I really had to laugh and I often reminded her of her part in denying me the chance to visit my team's stadium.

Another difficult situation developed that year for Lesley in relation to Colin's health. He was not one to complain or to go to the doctor but after we came back from our long haul holiday to New Zealand, which had been his dream location, he was absolutely exhausted. He still worked hard but tended to then not be fit to do anything else and I urged him to ask the doctor to do some checks into his general health. After tests and referral to a consultant it turned out that he needed to have two of his parathyroid glands removed because there were tumours which had been causing long-term damage due to them leaching calcium from the bones and silently beginning to calcify his kidneys. The surgery went well but he was very ill for a while afterwards and with his kidney function having dropped to only 18% we were really worried but trying to keep things positive for Lesley. Having to cancel our planned holiday on doctor's orders confirmed for her that her Dad was very poorly but she worked hard at keeping calm and was overjoyed when there was some improvement and her Dad eventually became more like his usual self. She could cope with him needing to have regular checks and blood tests because that had always been part and parcel of her own life.

It can't be over-emphasised how anything that disrupts normal routine is almost impossible for an autistic person to deal with without a great deal of patience, support and understanding. They can appear to be selfish, self-centred and lacking empathy or sympathy when in actual fact it is simply that their life needs stability to allow them to remain calm and stay happy. On the morning of Colin's operation when we were ready to leave for me to drive him to hospital, Lesley had one of her complete melt-downs and became totally enraged which was the last thing Colin needed. It was very difficult to deal with this but it was due to her inability to discuss how worried she was feeling and how terrified she was that I was taking her Dad away from her and not going to be bringing him back. When your own emotions are already heightened it can be very hard to cope with someone who seems to only be thinking of themselves but it is vital at such times to try not to force further confrontation and to allow time to pass for the emotions to settle before trying to talk things out. By the afternoon, Lesley was distraught at the impact of her behaviour and desperate for me to collect her to take her to see her Dad after his surgery. Regardless of how much she hurt me at times, it was always herself she hurt most and the days after such episodes would leave her wrung out emotionally and exhausted physically.

Even people dropping in unexpectedly at home to visit Colin or him having to spend extra time in bed on bad days was enough to make things hard for Lesley to handle but knowing that her Dad was home and would hopefully continue to improve gave her more motivation to cope. It was important to keep her focussed on the positives and to play down the negatives so that she felt things were moving in the right direction and we tended to depend a lot on humour to help. If there was laughter in the house, we were on the right track as far as Lesley was concerned and this saw us through the most difficult times over the years.

Difficult Times

Before Colin's illness I had decided to take early retirement from teaching to be able to give Lesley a bit more support. To get to her work she needed to take two buses in both directions and she was beginning to find this a bit too much particularly in bad weather. This would mean that she might need to give up her volunteering and the thought of all she would lose out on if this proved to be necessary made Colin and me evaluate what was most important to us. If I stopped working she would be able to get a lift to or from work every day – or both ways when it proved necessary. Her tiredness was continuing to be an issue and she simply didn't seem to have any reserves of energy. With this in mind, and with the period problems still being an issue, we also visited her GP to discuss whether anything could be done to help with the monthly problems which we felt were a huge factor in her lack of energy and which made life even more difficult for her to cope with.

The doctor said that there were a number of options available and that she would refer Lesley to the hospital. An appointment came quickly and Lesley was delighted to find that it was a young female doctor who discussed all the issues with both of us. The options were narrowed down to two possibilities for Lesley, an operation to remove all of the lining of the womb which would require a general anaesthetic or a hormone injection that should lead to the periods lightening considerably or even stopping. Lesley opted for the injection and we were very surprised to find that it could be given there and then. This meant that we hadn't had time to investigate it further but we both felt that it was an easier option than an operation and so we went to have it administered.

How wrong could we have been? I'm sure that for a great many people it is an ideal treatment that causes no real problems. However, for Lesley it was to be the start of the worst months of her life. We didn't initially think of the injection as being the trigger for the changes in Lesley and for some time we just thought that her mood was considerably worse. When she began to withdraw from everything that normally gave her pleasure in life, we realised that there was a very real problem. She stopped doing anything other than going to her work – and even with this she began to suggest taking time off, something she had never done. There was no music being played, no television watched, no time spent on the computer, no puzzles being attempted and no magazine being read. She didn't want to go out anywhere even for meals and in reality, we had lost our daughter.

Occasionally we still had a day where a rage would erupt but for the majority of the time she just became sadder, lower and more withdrawn. She would curl up in a chair and stare at the floor for hours and nothing we did reached her. My Mum commented on how difficult their Monday night chats had become and some of her friends spoke about the change in her at work. As Christmas week approached with Lesley slipping further down into the depths of despair I suggested that we needed to speak to a doctor and Lesley tearfully agreed. Sadly, the only appointment available was with the doctor who years previously had been very dismissive about medication being an option to help with Lesley's rages and this visit proved to be just as much of a let-down. He listened to everything we had to say and then told Lesley that he had a suggestion for her that should be of great help. She was to picture herself in a happy place which would stop her from getting too sad or too angry.

I waited for the next bit of advice or help but that was it. By this time, I had found out that some women reacted very badly to the injection Lesley had been given and that it could trigger depression but even mentioning this to the doctor got no reaction. We came out and both of us were near tears in the car because we had been pinning our hopes on there being something that could be done to help to turn things around. Lesley admitted that she felt scared about what was happening to her and she didn't know how to cope. Colin and I tried to tell her that maybe being on holiday from work and having time to rest and relax would help her but this gave her no comfort.

Christmas day that year was extremely difficult. We had my Mum with us as usual for our Christmas Dinner and we all worked hard at trying to pretend everything was fine but there was no joy in it for Lesley. At night we all went to my brother's house which was our usual routine too but Lesley said she was too tired to stay and she just wanted to get back home. She wanted to go straight to bed and though Colin and I tried to talk her round, we could see that it was pointless. Sadly, the next day was to be one of the worst of our lives.

Lesley was in a foul mood when she got up and nothing we said or did helped her in any way. She said that Christmas had been awful, she didn't know what was wrong with her but she hated her life and wished she was dead. Her rage mounted and it quickly went from continuously slamming doors, storming around and shouting at us to her having grabbed a carving knife in the kitchen and threatening to either use it on us or on herself. We were worried sick as this was a level of escalation we had never seen. When Lesley was in the grips of these rages she had almost super-human strength and we knew that if we tried to get the knife away from her we could cause a bigger problem. Talking did nothing to calm matters and we really didn't know what to do to try to help.

I decided that I had no option but to phone NHS 24 to ask a doctor for help but in my innocence I explained why I was so worried about her – and then discovered that if any violence was threatened the police had to be sent to investigate. I was devastated and said that this was not what we needed, that Lesley needed something that would help to bring her down to a calmer level, but there was no way around the issue. Through my tears I told Colin what was to happen and tried to explain to Lesley but she was still too wound up to take it in. It was only when the police car arrived with flashing blue lights that she realised what I had done and she flew to her room screaming that she hated me – but dropping the knife as she went.

Thankfully we got two sensitive officers who firstly checked that everyone in the house was all right before listening to what had led to my call. The female officer was calm, practical and mature and said immediately that this was not a 'normal' case of domestic violence or abuse. I was breaking my heart as I felt that I had betrayed Lesley but she assured me that while Lesley had to understand that what she had done was utterly wrong, she could see that there was a much bigger issue to be dealt with. She said that they could take Lesley to hospital and ask a doctor there to assess her – but that she would almost certainly be sent home and told to see her GP the next day which would not have helped how she was feeling that night and would be an experience that she could well do without.

She also said that in domestic violence cases they could take the person for a night in the cells – but that no one would dream of leaving someone as vulnerable as Lesley in a cell. We were terrified that this incident was going to lead to Lesley being charged in some way or having a police record but she reassured about this too. She suggested that if they could get Lesley to come through to sit with us all she would tell her that she was giving her an official warning – which would actually be meaningless – in the hope that this would shock Lesley into awareness of the seriousness of her actions and we agreed to try this.

Lesley listened. She looked absolutely shattered but was able to agree to what was being said to her and she promised that it would never happen again. She admitted that she just wasn't coping and the officer told her that she would have to go to see a doctor the next day as they would be putting in a report to social work telling them that this was an agreed next step. I said that we would never get an appointment at short notice and she said that I should go out for the surgery opening to tell them that it was an emergency and that Lesley had to be seen.

When the officers left, Lesley turned to me and very coldly said that she hated me and would never forgive me for what I had done and then she went to her room and refused to have anything to do with either of us, still obviously livid. We hadn't had anything to eat or drink all day and tried to get her to have something but she shouted her refusal and we felt that we were no further forward. I had moved all knives and sharp objects out of reach even though I don't think we really thought that this was a concern any more but we were devastated and very worried.

I phoned my brother who lived very close in case someone told them that they had seen a police car at our door for hours and he came along immediately with my sister-in-law. They were shocked and upset, even more so when it was obvious that Lesley still felt anger rather than remorse. I will always be grateful for what they did next because Kenny said that she had better pack an overnight bag right away because her Mum and Dad needed time to get over what had happened and she was to stay with them for the night. She refused at first but Kenny said that she had left us all with no option and that I would collect her when I had been to the doctor's surgery first thing the next morning.

I was given an appointment for quite early that morning and came back to get Lesley who was by then simply broken-hearted - and broken. She clung to me, full of regret and embarrassment and desperate to know that we still loved her. We went to see the doctor, thankfully Dr Kerr this time and managed to tell him what had happened. He asked Lesley lots of questions and she was able to tell him how she had been feeling over the previous weeks and how she just didn't know what was wrong with her. I told him all of the things that I had told the other doctor but this time he explained to Lesley that he thought she was a very poorly young lady. He was sure that she was suffering from depression with the occasional rages being part of her usual emotional difficulties but that she was going from extreme lows to the heights of the feelings of rage and that this was too much for her poor head to cope with. He stressed that it was an illness, that it was not her fault and that he would help her to get better.

He explained that she needed to keep taking her usual medication but that taking an anti-depressant as well would eventually help to balance things out until things settled. We returned home and she had a good cry when she saw her Dad. We talked about how devastated we had felt the day before but that it wasn't a case of forgiving Lesley, more a case of supporting her and helping her till she felt better. She agreed that she had to make big efforts too and that she would need to try to talk more about her feelings and be aware of days when her mood was worse. We all agreed that none of us could take a day like that again for any reason.

I'd love to say that there was an immediate change but life isn't like that. Lesley did improve a bit after a number of weeks but was still not like her usual self and did not want to do much. We went on holiday a few months later and for the first time ever Lesley did not get friendly with anyone and would only answer people with one word replies. It was like being on holiday with a stranger and we were quite concerned that away from her own environment we were seeing that she actually remained quite ill. There hadn't been any rages but the low mood and lack of interest in things was still very apparent.

She was due for her six-monthly blood tests when we came back and when we saw her lady doctor to discuss the results, she asked how Lesley was in general. We told her that although Lesley felt a bit better she was getting very little pleasure out of life and wasn't enjoying any of her usual interests. Her monthly problems hadn't even improved and the doctor showed a lot of care and concern. She agreed that it was probably necessary for Lesley to have the operation that had been mentioned previously since further injections were obviously not an option and then she also suggested that she ask someone with more experience in mental health issues to meet Lesley to ensure that the medication she was taking for the depression was right for her. The referrals were made with great success eventually gained from both.

The specialist talked with both of us for an hour and a half and she then took Lesley's hands and told her with great compassion that she was very sorry for how badly she had been affected by the depression but that she was making her a promise that things would get better. She explained that the dose of the medicine had been a starter level that should have been monitored and increased if it wasn't doing enough to help. This had somehow been missed but the doctor said that she would e-mail the surgery so that there would be a new prescription ready to be collected the next day. She talked to Lesley about dealing with the feelings of rage and suggested that she needed to work at finding ways to cope with this without letting it boil over in the house but that without the depression, that should be easier to deal with.

The GP asked to see Lesley to discuss the report and to further explain the new prescription. Within a couple of weeks on the increased medication we were amazed to begin to hear Lesley singing again to her music and to have her cracking jokes and discussing Coronation Street. She enjoyed going out for a cuppa and got chattier in company. It was such a relief after the previous seven or eight months which I wouldn't wish on my worst enemy and which gave us all such an insight into the dark world of real depression. Thankfully for us, it was successfully treated in Lesley and she was so grateful to be back feeling like she normally did and enjoying life again.

The other bonus was that the operation turned out to be the best thing that ever happened to Lesley - in her opinion. She sailed through it, going in fasted for the procedure first thing in the morning and getting home early in the afternoon. It took a few weeks for things to settle down completely, but after that she didn't have any further bleeding at all – and I think she celebrated this more than anything else as it made such a positive difference to her life.

Holidays in particular were greatly improved when she didn't have the fear of accidents in strange hotel beds and with her joy in travel returning, we planned a surprise trip for her. As well as her beloved Hibs, her other football love was Manchester United and this led to us having a wonderful few days away. There was a programme on television that Lesley enjoyed called 'Four in a Bed' with rival bed and breakfast establishments vying for the title of 'Best B & B'. She had been fascinated by a 'hobbit house' in Alderley Edge just outside Manchester and I planned a surprise trip to this fascinating little place.

We did tell Lesley that we had booked to stay there for a couple of nights and she was extremely excited about it but we didn't tell her that we had booked a stadium tour of Old Trafford and a meal in 'The Red Café' Manchester United's on-site restaurant. We did our usual planning of what we would do while we were away and I suggested, casually, that a trip into Manchester on the train might be a nice day out and we all agreed on this for the day after we arrived.

That morning we got the train in to the city and then I mentioned that we might consider making a trip on one of the trams and again we all agreed. I supposedly randomly chose a route and we discussed just staying on for a few stops and then getting off to explore. Of course Lesley had no idea that none of this was casual or un-planned and when we got off we knew what direction to head in. It was a wee bit further to walk than I had estimated but we knew we were getting close. Lesley was beginning to drag her feet a bit and asked what we thought we were going to see as it wasn't a very interesting area. I agreed, realising that the junction in front of us was just yards away from the stadium, and I told Colin that maybe we had walked far enough. Colin said we would have a look along the next road and if there was nothing much to see, we would just go to the next tram stop and head back to the city centre.

Seconds later, on passing the end of a huge warehouse type building, the stadium car park was in front of us, but Lesley didn't immediately notice where we were. I will never forget her face when she turned and saw the frontage of her 'Stadium of Dreams' and she looked at the grins on our faces before asking if we had known that Old Trafford was in the area. We laughed and told her that it had all been planned to let her see it but kept the suspense going for a bit longer by not letting her know we were going in.

Colin suggested that we walk right down through the car park to see the statues and the doorway up close and she readily agreed.

As we got close to the door, Colin said that you could probably only go further if you were booked to do a tour and Lesley agreed just as I was waving the tickets which had been hidden in my bag. I said that these might help and she shrieked with excitement and almost squeezed the breath out of us both. There followed a wonderful experience every minute of which she loved and it was great to see the joy on her face. You don't need to support Manchester United to be in awe of the set-up and the trophy room itself would have been worth the visit. The fact that we were also booked in for a meal was a huge bonus for Lesley and a great way to round off the day out. Again it was things like this that made up for the bad times and we celebrated being the happy Three Musketeers on Tour once more.

In April 2014 my nephew Calum and his fiancée Lorna were getting married and the anticipation of the big day was a roller coaster for Lesley. She didn't know whether to simply be excited about the big occasion or to be nervous because there would be lots of people there who were strangers to her. This was her usual reaction to anything social and we just had to keep reassuring her that it would be fine with all the focus on the bride and groom. She chose an outfit to wear and much to my surprise it had a skirt which she normally hated. Then the week before the wedding she decided that she couldn't handle wearing a skirt and we had a frantic search to find smart trousers with the elastic waist she needed to go with the purchased top that she did want to wear. Fortunately, this proved to be easier than we had expected and she was then comfortable with her appearance for the big day.

Our friend and hairdresser, Frances, had offered to do our hair and make sure our fascinators were firmly in place on the morning of the wedding. This proved to be just as well because I had been trying on my fascinator back to front until Frances put me right and this relaxed Lesley and allowed her to have a really good laugh at my expense. We arrived at New Lanark having all scrubbed up quite well and Lesley was in fine form. Kenny saw us arriving and made his usual cheeky comments to her and again had her laughing and looking forward to the ceremony. Lorna was stunning and Calum immaculate in his kilt outfit and the service was very relaxed and quite informal. Lesley had been worrying about the big tables for the dinner but there were no strangers at her table so she was very relieved and thoroughly enjoyed her meal sitting between her Dad and me.

She managed a few dances afterwards but was very pale and tired looking by then and she told me that she had a violent headache and couldn't cope with any more. Kenny and Annie had taken a cottage on site and had already said that if she needed a rest she could make use of it so I got the key and she rested on the sofa for a while. However, when I went back to see how she was she said that she just couldn't cope with staying and really wanted to get home so we said thank you to everyone and headed home telling her that she had done really well all day and not to worry about leaving early. She slept in the car on the way back and was extremely tired the next day but quite proud that she had lasted so well and she had loved being part of her cousin's big day as this was the first of her immediate family to get married since Kenny and Annie's big day with her as Flower Girl.

Devastation

We had noticed on a recent week's holiday to Tunisia that Lesley was needing to sleep more and more and following this many days would have her going for a sleep when I brought her home from work in the afternoon only to need to be in bed before nine o'clock, utterly exhausted. This pattern continued and by the time the May Bank Holiday was due, I was talking about it being good for her to have a long weekend for a bit of a rest. Colin had to work on the holiday Monday but I was free to do anything that Lesley felt up to.

We had our usual Friday meeting at the speedway and it was a particularly good night with a lot of banter in the crowd around us which Lesley loved. On the way back home she told us that she had decided to take us out for Sunday lunch, that it was to be her treat and she wasn't taking no for an answer. We had a laugh about this and asked her if she had won the lottery but she said she just wanted to do it and she chose where she wanted to go. She would sometimes treat us to coffees out or pay for the drinks if we were out for a meal but this time she wanted to do it all even though it wasn't a special occasion.

On the Saturday morning we all went to a garden centre for some things I needed and enjoyed a coffee together. She had a rest on the Saturday afternoon and we relaxed together watching television at night. We were very surprised when 'Papa's Pooch' was brought through for a cuddle and I asked if she was feeling a bit low as the cuddly toy hadn't appeared in the living room for months. She said that she felt fine but she just needed to hold it for a while and enjoy the cuddle. Lesley always needed lots of cuddles, they seemed to reassure her and she would often kneel by my chair for a long hug with me getting a mouthful of hair as part of the experience.

She went to bed very happily that night saying how much she was looking forward to going out for lunch and having her favourite sticky toffee pudding. As I've mentioned before, it was a standing joke when we had a meal out that Lesley would have a starter and a main course and on being offered a dessert, would initially say no thanks. We would then act surprised and ask if she was feeling poorly due to her turning down her favourite course and she would then respond by saying 'Oh all right then' as if she was doing us a favour and just forcing herself to eat it. The little restaurant she'd chosen served delicious sticky toffee pudding so there was no question that she would be having it – and indeed it was the reason for her choice of venue. We all enjoyed our meal and headed for home where Lesley again had a rest in the afternoon. Later I asked her if she had thought of what she would like to do on her Monday off and she replied immediately that she would like me to take her and her Nana out for a run in my new car and she would buy the coffees wherever we went. I suggested that she might like to do something just for herself but she was adamant that her Nana hadn't been in the new wee purple car that Lesley loved so she phoned and made the arrangements.

Again she wanted to pay and said that she had enough money in her 'extras' even though she had footed the bill for lunch the day before. She was delighted that her Nana liked being in my new car and we had a lovely relaxing trip. It annoyed her, with her sense of fairness, that her Dad had missed out due to being at work so she bought him a Mars Bar to make up for missing a cake which delighted him when she gave it to him that night. We all said that it had been a particularly enjoyable weekend and Lesley seemed refreshed and very perky.

She was quite excited about the Tuesday because Audrey from the Befrienders organisation had contacted her to ask her to attend a meeting in the afternoon in Bathgate. She had something to discuss with Lesley and had invited her to meet for a coffee. I arranged to pick her up from her work and take her over to Bathgate and said I would wait for her and take her home. When I arrived to collect her she came out with a chocolate Flake for me to show how much she appreciated me being her chauffeur in 'Mum's Taxi' and we had a laugh about this as we headed to meet Audrey. I had a walk around the shops and then just waited in the car till she returned – and she had another laugh when I admitted that I had already eaten the Flake though she said I deserved it.

Lesley was on cloud nine because she had been presented with a certificate to recognise the fact that her and Jillian had been in the Befriending together for over ten years – and what delighted her more was that Jillian was going to be presented with an award. She couldn't wait to show the certificate to her Dad and tell him about it.

Early that evening Colin and I were going out for an hour to a weekly dance class that we had just started and she was winding us up about the fact that we had been falling out over the Cha-Cha the week before and told us to behave ourselves when we were out. She was delighted when we returned and showed her how good we had become with the dance and she said that she thought we were nearly ready for Strictly Come Dancing. Hibs were playing a game that night and the result was crucial due to their relegation battle. Lesley had her radio on with the ear-plugs in to listen to their progress but as the game approached the final stages it was obvious that her team were not going to do the business. She went to get ready for bed but instead of listening to the end of the match she decided just to go to bed. I asked if she wanted me to come and tell her when the final whistle went but she admitted that she was feeling very tired and just wanted to settle down.

We got our usual hugs and she said 'Night, night, love you both lots, see you in the morning,' as she always did and we hugged her back, said it was a pity about the football and told her we loved her too. I was taking her to work in the morning and I suggested that she could have a bit of a long lie so as long as she was up and ready she wouldn't need to be through for breakfast until around ten to eight. Colin wasn't working on the Wednesday and he was going to have a gentle start to his day too so she went off delighted with the plan.

Next morning, I got up, went to the toilet and then went through to the kitchen to organise the breakfast as usual. I had told Colin to sleep a bit longer and it was only when I realised that Lesley should have been through that I went to tell her to hurry. When I saw that her bedroom door was still closed I was surprised. Lesley never slept in and it would only be maybe once in a year that she needed to be wakened and even if she needed to be up very early she would set her alarm and be up. I went in just saying her name quietly so as not to give her a fright but she didn't react. She was lying as she always did, on her front with her head turned to the side and the covers right up to her neck. I walked to her bedside repeating her name a bit louder and then gently touching her shoulder when she still didn't respond. Her face was turned to the other side and I ran around her bed by this time shouting her name in fear but my wonderful, unique, precious, beloved daughter had gone. I pulled the covers back and her mottled arms confirmed what my mind didn't want to take in. I ran for Colin who had just wakened with my shouting and I had to tell him that our lovely Lesley had died in her sleep.

This is so hard to write as it feels like it is happening again and the pain, shock and utter devastation is just as raw more than a year later. Colin was distraught and unbelieving – it just didn't feel possible that this could have happened. It was like being in the middle of the worst nightmare ever but there was no chance of waking up with any feeling of relief. I phoned 999 on automatic pilot but I'm not even sure if I was coherent. Eventually I was made aware that an ambulance had been dispatched and they told me to make sure the door was open for their arrival. Colin was out at the front gate when he saw the ambulance but they came to the back door and it must have been awful for them because of the state we were both in.

The two men came to Lesley's room and then I think one of them asked us to leave them to check Lesley and suggested that I should phone someone to come to support us. I phoned Kenny but again I don't think I was even making sense and what a dreadful thing it was to tell him on the phone. He said he would be there as soon as possible and he was true to his word, having also collected Annie and brought her too.

The police had to be sent for due to this being a sudden unexplained death but I was allowed to stay with Lesley most of the time which was all I wanted. I can't say it was unreal because we were only too aware of what we were facing but there was a level of peace as long as I could hold her hand and stroke her hair and it almost kept the reality away. The rest of the day passed in a painful blur. The two young police officers, Kat and Shaun, treated us with such compassion that I will never forget them. They had to ask so many questions and Colin in particular kept going off at tangents because he needed them to know about our Lesley as the lovely person she was in life. He showed them photographs because, he said, they weren't seeing her at her best and he needed them to know what she was really like. He shared stories to make her real to them and I don't know how they maintained their professionalism in the midst of our grief and shock. They explained that CID would also need to come as a matter of course and that Lesley would then need to be taken away.

Kenny and Annie had gone to break the news to my Mum but I didn't want her to have to come and sit through the police interviews. The young officers said they would let us know when the CID officers would be coming so that we could get my Mum down before they arrived and we did this. What a dreadful thing for a grandparent to have to deal with the death of their first grandchild. Kenny had also phoned in to Lesley's work for me as soon as I realised that they would be worried about her not being in on time and he told the rest of the family too and spoke to Colin's boss and informed the undertaker, Jim Brodie. I think he was also dealing with the police at times as a sergeant had arrived and liaised with Kenny rather than us as it was Kat and Shaun's duty to conduct the proceedings. They were also telling Kenny what needed to happen so that he could be of support to us and we'll never repay him for his strength that day in spite of his own grief at the loss of 'his wee pal'.

Two CID officers came in the afternoon and introduced themselves very formally and with a coldness that was probably necessary for them to be able to do their jobs. I remember reacting to the senior officer when he bluntly asked where 'the body' was. I told him that my daughter's name was Lesley and that she was in her bedroom and I think my comment hit home because he showed more warmth and consideration afterwards. When they had completed their assessment, and spoken with the two young officers and the senior officer they confirmed that they were now arranging for Lesley to be taken to Edinburgh. I was quite upset about this as I hadn't realised that she wouldn't just stay locally but the senior officer then redeemed himself in my eyes. He had obviously seen all the Hibs things in Lesley's room and he must have had some personal knowledge because he explained to Colin that Lesley was going to the Cowgate in Edinburgh. This was where a priest originally founded Hibernian back in 1875 and it helped me to come to terms with where she was going and it meant a lot to Colin. She had to be taken to Edinburgh when she was born so there was a sad symmetry in her being taken there now.

The young police officers, who had been with us since morning, said that they would escort her there and this meant such a lot to us. Some other family members had arrived and paid their respects before she needed to leave and I had time again to just sit with her till Kenny told me it was time to say goodbye. We had to leave the room and all go into our bedroom with the door shut to allow them to take her from her home and it was simply beyond bearing. I could never have known that pain such as this existed and wouldn't want my worst enemy to suffer this level of grief and loss.

I knew that we needed to start to let people know what had happened but we decided that only the most important contacts would be made that night, people who might hear from others if we didn't get in touch first. The most important outside the family were Janette and Rod and I geared myself up to make the call. As my best friend from schooldays and Lesley's Godmother, I knew Janette would be devastated. There was no one at home and I just left a message as calmly as I could to ask her to phone when she got home. She later told me that she could sense from my tone that there was something wrong and was dreading returning the call – but would never for a moment have imagined what I was going to tell her. They came straight up to see us as the good friends they have always been and supported us through the days that lay ahead. June and Kenny our friends from Armadale also came as soon as we let them know. Mary, the secretary at Lesley's work came to hand in flowers and to let us know that they had told the other volunteers, Lesley's friends. Mary was due to be going away on holiday and wanted to see us before she went to let us know that everyone was broken-hearted and utterly shocked at the loss of our Lesley and that they were all thinking of us.

One of the most difficult calls was to Lynne and Frank but it had to be done that night as we knew that the news would probably filter out to Whitburn quite quickly. Their loss of their youngest son Craig in a car accident some years previously meant that they would know what we were facing but it would also be devastating for them to hear our bad news and re-live their darkest days. Lynne could scarcely speak but said they would come out the next night and their empathy was so real. I was only too aware of the dreadful journey they had been on since losing Craig and they knew the devastation that faced us.

I didn't want to tell Leigh on the phone but Annie offered to take me out to see her the following day to speak to her in person. Sadly, by the time we tracked her down – she was out shopping - she had already heard. We were amazed to discover that a chain of phone calls had taken place the night before which ended in Leigh being told by one of her other friends. Similarly, one of my friends, miles away in South Queensferry already knew when I phoned her – bad news really does get around quickly.

When everyone left that first night and Colin and I were left on our own, the reality hit hard. We were simply broken and lost and hurting more than words can say. Eventually we decided that we should go to bed but I found that as soon as I turned the light out I was in a state of total panic – I couldn't bear the darkness, maybe because it symbolised the light having gone out of my life. I thought Colin was sleeping and I crept out of bed only to be followed by him minutes later. Neither of us could settle at all so we just spent the whole night talking.

We talked about how this was not how we had imagined life would turn out, how we had tried so hard to plan and prepare for the time when Lesley would be left without us so that she would be financially secure and supported by social services. I found one thought to cling on to in the darkest moments and it is all that has sustained me since. Lesley dreaded the thought of being on her own and she feared greatly, as I did, for how her quality of life would be if she didn't have us. I suddenly knew with certainty that if she had been offered a choice of living for twenty years after we had gone or having to die young herself, her choice would have been to go first. She had a good, full life and she got lots of pleasure and happiness from her family, friends, her work and her interests but she found life hard to cope with and needed a lot of support. She often said to me that she didn't know what she would do without me and I know she looked on me as the most vital part of her ability to cope with life, so her worries were justified. At least I could try to comfort myself with the thought that she would never suffer the pain of loss that we were feeling and she would never be left lonely without us. She was only 35 years old but her poor body had been through so much and we also realised that night that the terrible tiredness had probably been a sign that she was simply running down.

Sad Plans

Having breakfast without her in the morning was awful and the thought of beginning to plan her funeral was almost surreal. When we had updated our wills, and set up the trust a few years earlier we had also looked again at some of our funeral details. We all had pre-paid funerals which I had organised after my own cancer diagnosis to make life easier for Colin if I didn't make it. I had already written all the information for the person who would take each of our services thinking that this would save Lesley from any hassle if she was being left alone. However, I felt very strongly that due to Lesley not being at all religious, I did not want a traditionally religious goodbye for her, it needed to be more personal.

I had known Jim Brodie, the local undertaker, all his life and I knew he would be very helpful and supportive. He was able to put us in touch with Lesley Fraser, a wonderful lady who was more than happy to give us the service – and tribute – that we needed and she came to discuss everything with us. She was willing to use my pre-written 'script' as the basis of the service and was also in agreement when I said that I wanted to speak about my beloved daughter. We explained that we did not want things to be overtly religious and she drew up her plans giving us choices every time she was going to use a verse or a quote so the service could be as fitting as possible.

When Jim came back to finalise details once Lesley had been brought back to the parlour in Harthill, he realised that although my plans had been meticulous we were short of one piece of music for a time of quiet reflection during the service at the crematorium. He said that we didn't need to worry, we still had plenty of time to choose – but then he took his phone out and said that he had a favourite song that seemed very fitting due to some of the things we had already told him. It was Annie Lennox singing 'Into the West' and when Jim left we got it on the computer and listened to the words which turned out to be simply perfect. Probably the most moving part of the song for us came in the last verse which reads:

Hope fades into the world of night.
Through shadows falling, out of memory and time
Don't say: 'We have come now to the end'
White shores are calling, you and I will meet again.
And you'll be here in my arms, just sleeping

The thought of the word 'Hope' featuring in this beautiful song meant the world to us – our baby's middle name given to her when everything looked black and hopeless. That Hope had seen us through so much and now it would be a part of her final tribute.

This song still moves me to tears but we were happy that everything we had chosen to include would have met with Lesley's approval and this gave us immense comfort as the long days passed till the day of the funeral ten days after Lesley's death.

During that time, I lost track of all the people who made the effort to come to see us, most of them utterly shocked and many of them truly devastated. When I was making phone calls to break the news I think almost all of them thought I was going to say that my 'bad news' was about Colin, knowing that his health was not great. No one was prepared for what I was going to tell them and we will always appreciate the support and care that was shown to us, and more importantly, we loved those who came and shared their particular memories of our girl.

We began to realise something that Lesley would never have believed. She had been a total inspiration to a great many people, even some who scarcely knew her. Her beautiful, warm smile was mentioned again and again, but her good manners, her caring and her friendly nature had all made people admire her in every walk of her life. The house became like a florist's shop – vases had to be borrowed and the flowers took over the whole living room and kitchen. There were hundreds of cards, letters, phone calls and texts from people who just wanted to let us know they cared and I will always be grateful to those who actually came to visit when they must have been wondering what sort of atmosphere they would be entering. The good thing for us all was that it meant there was time to share memories and experiences of how Lesley had touched each life and she would have been amazed and saying 'all this for me?'

There were some beautiful comments in the cards and letters too which showed how much people had thought of our daughter. Andrew, who had been her boss up until the year before she died, sent a card with a picture of a dandelion seed head on it. Inside he had written 'Like the pappus of the dandelion, Lesley parachuted down to us all those years ago, to enrich, enliven and enlighten our understanding of life and disability. I will always remember her friendly smiling face and the happy times.' Audrey from the Befrienders wrote 'Lesley brightened the world around her with her beautiful smile and sense of fun. We are all better for knowing her.' The staff at Autism Initiatives wrote 'We all feel privileged to have known Lesley - she faced the world with such courage and good humour.' Our old neighbours, Lorna and John wrote 'We feel honoured to have had Lesley in our lives - we will never forget her'. Margaret Cook, Lesley's nursery teacher wrote 'Lesley was such a lovely, loving child and a caring adult.' Jillian, her befriender wrote 'Lesley was an amazing person. I am proud and happy to have known her. She enriched my life so much.' Kenny and Annie put 'A special wee pal who grew into a loving and caring young woman, deeply missed, loved forever, her hugs treasured forever.' My Mum wrote 'Take heart from knowing that while she was with you she was surrounded by love.'

Many people mentioned how special she was and how she touched people's hearts and our pride was probably in equal measure to our grief at this point. We so wanted to believe that somewhere, Lesley was smiling and enjoying the accolades in her own very modest way.

Colin phoned Dave who, with his wife Karen and their family, Billy and his family and Liz and Kenny and their family had been Colin and Lesley's main friends at the football over many years. They were shocked to hear the news and when Colin asked them to give a wee thought for Lesley at the game on the Saturday Dave immediately said they would do better than that. He said they would get flowers to take to the stadium and leave them at the East Stand in memory of 'Lovely Lesley' as Dave called her. This touched Kenny so much that he ended up going with Annie - him a Rangers fan and Annie not even liking football - to the Hibs match too and taking flowers from them, my Mum and us to add to the tribute there.

I have always been a very strong person and with the funeral to focus on, I more or less managed to keep things together in these early days and did what had to be done. Colin could scarcely speak without dissolving but the support of friends and family was a huge help. Kenny tended to be our rock and I think he would have done anything for us. Although Pete had never been close to us, he also got very involved in the first week and I think he just looked at Colin, who had aged so much, and wondered how, as a loving Dad, such a situation could be handled at all.

We hoped that someone from Hibs and someone from The Monarchs could manage to attend the funeral in respect of Lesley's passion and dedication for her two teams and Pete offered to go to Hibs and try to arrange something with them. He took a photograph of Lesley with him in case people didn't know who he was talking about, but it proved to be unnecessary as she was so well known. He had a meeting with the Chairman, Rod Petrie, and it was Rod himself who came to Harthill to represent the club, a huge gesture made even bigger by the fact that as a member of the Scottish Football Association Board he should already have been at Hampden for the Cup Final that day. He also got a strip and took it around all the players so that it could then be sent to Colin and he had beautiful flowers sent from the club. The club was further represented by a previous director, Dougie Cromb, coming to the crematorium in spite of his age and frailty. We had always kept in touch with Dougie from the days of his coming to Lesley's eighteenth birthday party and we were very touched that he made the trip through to pay his respects and talk of how he would never forget her.

I contacted The Monarchs and they immediately made announcements on the website, put a tribute to Lesley with a photograph on the main web page and had an entry in the programme about her loss. This meant that not only did our own wee crowd from Friday nights at Armadale attend the funeral, other fans from her broader circle of acquaintances and two directors came too. Lesley's hero, captain of the team Derek

Sneddon, paid a personal tribute which would have meant the world to her. There were tributes on the Voluntary Sector Gateway and Disability West Lothian websites, the Monarchs Chatzone and the Emmerdale's Speedway Fans forums too. We were stunned and moved by the level of acknowledgement of our loss of a very special person and for the display of esteem for Lesley that was being shown by so many people.

For ten days, we just seemed to be making tea for the constant stream of visitors and we were lucky if I managed to have a pot of soup on the go to have something hot to eat quickly when we got the chance. I remember one day of feeling that we needed just to 'be' for a wee while and just as some visitors left and I was heating soup, I was aware of another car arriving. I felt so guilty at thinking 'oh no' and then delighted to realise that it was Janette just popping in again to check on us. She joined us in some lunch and we had a couple of hours of being able to relax and talk without needing to have our public faces in place. Janette supported us both a great deal.

The people who came to see us helped us immensely, giving us a chance to talk about Lesley and reflect on her life and we will always be grateful to all those who made the effort. Some people found the visit harder to make than others though I imagine everyone dreaded seeing us beforehand. Lynnette, Lesley's friend from the speedway who had become her close friend over the years, came with her Dad, Bill who had always been close to Lesley and who gave her a big hug every Friday night. Lynnette was distraught and didn't think she could face coming to the house like she had done so often in the past, but this time with no Lesley. Yet she came and there were tears and laughter as we reminisced during the visit which probably helped us all. Lynnette was very worried about coping with the funeral and I think it probably helped a lot that she had already spent time with us before facing the visit to the crematorium.

Lesley was brought back to Harthill on the Monday evening and we arranged to go to the parlour the next morning. It had been agreed by all three of us that we would not want anyone to see us in our coffins after death and we kept this promise to Lesley even though part of us just wanted to hold her again. However, her own bed was a much better last memory and all we wanted to do was spend some time sitting with her in the room. Jim Brodie had been wonderful and was happy to dress Lesley as I wanted. She was to wear her favourite Monarchs t-shirt and the lovely new black palazzo style trousers that she had got for Calum's wedding and which had only been worn that day. A Hibs hat, not to be worn, but just there to represent her beloved Hibees was included and another more awkward request for Jim to deal with. If Hibs were playing, Lesley always wore her 'lucky green knickers'. I couldn't count how many pairs of these were hunted down over the years with various shades of green being acceptable. Jim, to his credit, didn't even blink when I told him about this and he also willingly agreed to taking some dry shampoo to freshen her hair and to use her favourite 'Charlie' body spray.

This all gave me a sense of fulfilling wishes that Lesley might have made herself and when we went to the funeral parlour, we felt at peace that we had continued to meet Lesley's needs. It was incredibly moving when we were shown into the room to find that they had sprayed some of the 'Charlie' perfume and it really felt as though she was with us and that the Three Musketeers were still strong.

We had decided to ask people, if they felt comfortable with it, to wear something to recognise Lesley's love of football and speedway for the funeral rather than just having blackness, which she would have hated. Pete went and got Hibs ties for him, Kenny and Colin to wear – a huge gesture for my blue-nose Rangers fanatical brothers to make. There were also Hibs lapel badges that the women could wear. Janette told us that Rod had gone to Edinburgh not even knowing where the stadium was and assuming that a sports shop would stock Hibs merchandise. Unfortunately, you have to buy directly from the club so he got a taxi and went to the stadium to buy a scarf and tie so that he too could pay his respects.

Colin wanted to wear a black suit and white shirt and was grateful to have the tie which he wore along with his Hibs tartan scarf in tribute to his 'Hibee Pal'. I decided to wear the dark green suit I had but hidden underneath would be Lesley's Manchester United strip with my Monarch's scarf on top. As it turned out on the day there were people wearing green for Hibs or blue for the Monarchs as well as any number of different football scarves and ties from throughout Scotland – and yet it was all utterly respectful and something Lesley would have loved.

We had made every arrangement carefully and with great thought and consideration and felt we were prepared for what lay ahead. Colin, Pete, Kenny, Janette and I were going to escort Lesley into the crematorium and we would each have a flower to leave with her. My Mum would also have a flower and would step forward from her seat in the front row to add her tribute when we arrived. Colin would place his last and I would keep mine until after my eulogy. Lesley's coffin would be adorned with her Hibs, Monarchs and Manchester United scarves and there would be a smiling photograph of her. There was also a late addition from Kenny who placed his Rangers 'Simply the Best' scarf with the others and she would have so appreciated the meaning behind that.

The service at Harthill in the parlour first should have prepared us for this being a much bigger occasion than we had expected as there were people having to stand inside and outside. When we came out and headed for Livingston the main street was at a standstill and we were extremely moved when Jim stopped the hearse for a few moments outside our house so that Lesley could have a final goodbye to her home. By the time we arrived at the crematorium, there was a sea of people trying to make their way in and it turned out that hundreds of people had turned out to show their respect for our beloved daughter.

As well as all of her family there were people from every walk of her life attending her tribute – teachers and pupils from Nursery, Primary and Secondary school as well as staff and students from her college years. Her friends and work colleagues, neighbours past and present, our family friends and our work colleagues, the sporting contingent – all thronged together to honour a very special young lady. Some people had made huge efforts to be there coming from as far afield as Newcastle and Montrose, Troon and Leith. We had seen Melissa who had been Lesley's key worker at Autism Initiatives during the year she had been with them on Tuesday afternoons. She was with some of the other staff members and we were grateful to them for coming. It was only later when she came to take her leave after the tea that we discovered she had recently moved away and was now living and working in Newcastle. She had driven up on her own just to pay her respects to Lesley because she had been so fond of her. Such gestures meant the world to us that day. Amy who had been Lesley's neighbour and childhood friend had driven up from Troon with her boyfriend who had never even met any of us, again showing such regard for our daughter.

To share the emotions of the day I include the words I had written, the first part delivered by Lesley Fraser and the second part by me.

The Life Story of Lesley McRobb

Lesley was born in 1978 - the much-wanted and much-loved only child of Beth and Colin. Being born with Apert's Syndrome, her start in life was difficult and it really didn't look possible that she would live. She was transferred from Bangour to Edinburgh with Colin and Lesley's Papa following the ambulance at high speed. Beth was devastated that she had to stay behind, but before they left she asked if Lesley could have a middle name added to her incubator – Hope. It was all there was to cling to on that first Sunday. The internal problems turned out to be not as severe as had been thought and her heart issues seemed to have been the result of the difficult birth, so amazingly she got home just over a week later. A lot of her first year of life was spent in the Southern General Hospital in Glasgow undergoing major surgery. These and later operations at Canniesburn were to give her the best chance to develop and enjoy as good a quality of life as possible.

In her early years, Lesley was a confident, sociable child who loved to get out and about. She always found her own way to sort out her physical difficulties – like dropping her feet behind the pedals on her bike if her hands couldn't pull the brakes hard enough. You should have seen the bruises on her shins! She was willing to have a go at anything – something which her Mum encouraged even when her Dad was more inclined to want to protect her. She did abseiling, mountain biking and kayak canoeing before either of her parents had ever tried these activities – and the fact that she overturned the canoe, falling in the water, didn't detract from the pleasure one bit!

Probably Lesley's finest childhood hour was being chosen, at six years old, to be the Rainbow Fairy Queen in Whitburn Gala Day – an experience she loved and the best and proudest day of her Mum's life. Her smile lasted for the whole of the parade in spite of a rather grey and cold June day and she waved to everyone at both sides of the street all the way around. She also loved being a Brownie and subsequently a Guide and the chance to go camping was always a bonus for her – even when the weather was poor she had a ball. Lesley was awarded the Baden Powell award for Guiding in recognition of all she achieved as a Guide in Whitburn.

It wasn't till she was 12 years old that she developed an interest in her Dad's football team – Hibs – and this was to prove to be a real passion for her. Over the years she collected hundreds of Hibs players' autographs and watched them play all over the country and at Hampden where she saw them win the League Cup in 2007 – one of her best days ever and her Dad's fondest memory. Her knowledge of the game and her ability to remember past players' names was incredible and her Dad couldn't have had a better partner to go to matches with. She developed another love which she shared with both of her parents – Speedway Racing at Armadale where she watched her beloved Monarchs in action. The family also supported the team when they raced at Glasgow, Berwick, Workington and Newcastle and victorious National League titles were the highlight of a few seasons. Dozens more autographs of Speedway riders joined the Hibs collection over the years.

By her early teens Lesley had become shy and self-conscious and life became more difficult for her. After she left school she attended West Lothian College followed by a training course and then she signed up for the Prince's Trust. This was to lead to her getting a voluntary work placement with Disability West Lothian, first in Bathgate and then at Carmondean in Livingston where she was a most reliable worker for over 14 years. Lesley scarcely missed a day in the office where she would do typing, answer the phone or do messages for other workers. She developed friendships with some of the other volunteers – Moira, Fraser, Gordon, Emma and Jacqui - which helped her to move on from the social problems that she had encountered at school.

Monday nights were always spent dining with her Nana and she liked to make sure that the meal she had at Mill Road was better than the one she had missed at home. On her Friday off she always visited her friend Leigh and sometimes they would go to Livingston together or go out for a meal. Eventually the two of them were encouraged by Beth to try going away together for a long weekend holiday break. They loved it and this was followed by a couple of Urquhart Tours.

Lesley's social opportunities were further improved when she agreed to find out about having a Befriender. She was lucky enough to be linked with Jillian and they hit it off immediately, leading to ten years of lovely meals out, cinema trips, bowling events or runs in the car. Thanks to Jillian, Lesley got some days or nights out without having to depend on her mum and dad and she loved this. They looked on each other as simply friends and the formal Befriending structure was only a small part of their relationship.

Lesley enjoyed spending time in her own room at home too where her computer and her music collection were her pride and joy. She had hundreds of CDs and particularly loved 60s and 70s music. She didn't go anywhere without her favourite selections on an MP3 player so that she was never without music, whether in cars, buses, planes or trains. Her Mum had taught her to type before she went to school so that she would have a back-up skill if handwriting was too tiring for her. However, the computer skills she developed went far beyond simple typing and her typing speed, considering she had no individual fingers, was incredible. She was a fan of Coronation Street from an early age and subscribed to the Inside Soap magazine so that she was always first in the know about breaking storylines. A trip to the Granada studios many years ago, was a huge success. She also subscribed to the Puzzle

Book magazine as she loved doing word puzzles and took these with her around the world on holiday.

In spite of her social limitations, Lesley loved going away on holiday with her Mum and Dad and she travelled all over the world to every continent. She particularly loved cruising where the planned, structured events and good food suited her and where she loved the fact that everything was on hand without having to do a lot of walking. Her all-time favourite holiday was to Borneo – a trip that was really made so that her Mum could see the orang utans but where Lesley simply fell in love with the beautiful, warm, friendly people and the incredible setting of the Nature Reserve where they stayed. If it had been closer to Scotland she would have gone back every year – she really did have very good taste!

Lesley's physical, social and emotional needs made life very difficult for her but throughout her life she remained a loving, loyal, kind and caring person who was spoken of as having a lovely friendly smile for anyone she met when she was out and about. Lesley's achievements in life, considering her limitations, were exceptional and she truly justified the early work the surgeons did to give her a life.

It doesn't seem fair that she only had 35 years but at least there is the comfort that she simply slept away in her own bed, peacefully and without any pain and she never needed to face life without her Mum and Dad in her corner.

Thanks for the Memories, Lovely Lesley

I hope I can be strong enough to say what I want to say for our beloved Lesley. This is not a day that any of us here would have wanted to be sharing – but your attendance shows how much you thought of our Les - and I thank you from Colin and me for supporting us and helping us to get through it.

When Lesley was born, it did not look as if she would make it at all and I vowed to her then that if she lived, I would always be there for her and that she would experience everything in life that her Dad and I could offer her. I'm proud to say that vow was carried out.

We just simply loved her – through good times and bad – and we can't really see a way forward without her right now. However, we have so many memories of her which will eventually let us grieve for her loss but celebrate the person she was – and we are so proud to have been her parents. People have said that we were a special family. Well, Colin and I are just ordinary – it was Lesley who was the special one. We always called ourselves 'The Three Musketeers' but now there are just two of us left.

Her family came first with her. She adored Colin and me with a love that was special and pure. There were many difficult times in our house but that love never wavered and she told us every single day how much we meant to her. She never once went to bed without telling us both that she loved us lots and she was reassured daily by our responses that we loved her too. She also dearly loved her Nana and never really got over losing her Papa.

Kenny and Annie were very special to her - Kenny was more than an uncle, he was her special pal as she grew up. There are also many friends here today who were considered like family by Lesley and who had a special place in her heart.

Considering all her problems she packed a lot into her 35 years. Her Uncle Pete asked us last week, if we could think back to when she was born, could we ever have imagined the journey she would have taken and the experiences she would have crammed in – and it just wouldn't have seemed remotely possible.

She visited every continent. She stood on the Great Wall of China; she went down into the depths of the Great Pyramid in Giza; she stood on the top of the Corcovado Mountain in Brazil; she fell in love with a Koala called Basil in Australia, a baby orang utan called Ten-Ten in Borneo and two elephants called Nandy and Tandy in South Africa.

She was there when her beloved Hibs won the League Cup in 2007 and when The Mighty Monarchs lifted their first ever Speedway league title in 2003 – and the ones that followed. She was also a big Manchester United fan and was thrilled to have a Manchester United Stadium tour to see all the trophies that she had watched them win on television. Actually football was the cause of some splits in the McRobb household due to me being a blue-nose and Chelsea fan and although Lesley and her Dad were bosom buddies when it came to Hibs, Colin was a Liverpool fan. However, Lesley only ever wanted us all to be happy on a

Saturday night – so she would have accepted draws every time the rivals met – unlike her Dad! Football and Speedway were her passions in life – and she would be amazed today to see my two blue-nose brothers choosing to wear Hibs ties in her honour – and those who know them will appreciate what a tribute to Lesley that really is.

She met lots of celebrities – winning a champagne afternoon tea with Jason Donovan in London just last year and being good enough to take me with her. Her autograph collection of football, speedway and entertainment stars runs into hundreds. Colin got to dread new Hibs signings because he had to make sure that she met them all and that she had every current manager and players' signatures in her collection.

Yet she was shy and self-conscious and would never have boasted or bragged about any of it. She was kind and caring and loving and loyal. She was generous of spirit and had manners which were impeccable. She appreciated the little things and thanked you for anything you did for her. For those who really knew her she had a wicked sense of humour and she loved a laugh - especially if it was at her Dad's expense because their humour was so similar.

She touched people's hearts and made them smile and the fact that you have come here today means that she touched you too. She deserves to be remembered fondly and we hope you will keep her in your hearts. I'm sure that somewhere she is watching and smiling and enjoying the fact that so many people came to say goodbye. I doubt if she could have had any idea of the huge hole she would leave behind that just cannot be filled. So many people have talked to us about her beautiful smile – that she was a ray of sunshine and a lesson to us all.

Our brightest light has gone out and our lives will be dimmer from now on. I might walk in the sun again but my wee shadow has gone. We will treasure everything she did to enrich our lives while we had her with us and we hope she will walk beside us as we face life without her. Sleep well my baby – your Dad and I will always love you.

I was so relieved to have managed to read everything at both services without breaking down and as I turned to place my flower on Lesley's coffin and say my last goodbye, I was incredibly moved to hear spontaneous applause from all those gathered in the crematorium. All those sitting and standing inside and those who were outside hearing the service through speakers joined together and it was a very special moment. Gratefully I clung to Colin's hand as I re-joined him for the rest of the service.

We had carefully chosen the music for the service too. 'This Little Light of Mine' because it was her childhood favourite and she was a shining light; Sunshine on Leith, the Proclaimers Hibs anthem; Ronan Keating's 'If Tomorrow Never Comes' because Lesley and I loved it and the words meant a lot; 'One More Step' her favourite from Guiding days and because she was moving to her new world; Annie Lennox 'Into the West' for the words and the spirit of the story it tells; 'Auld Lang Syne' to finish because Lesley loved it at the end of an occasion and because we wanted to try to draw everyone together before we left. There were also some beautiful verses that Lesley Fraser had helped us to choose and all of them had real meaning, nothing at all was included unless it 'fitted'. Our favourite verse tied in so well with the Annie Lennox song which was written for the 'Lord of the Rings' films:

In a similar way, we may sit and watch someone we love quietly slipping away until in the end we say, 'There, she's gone,' as a ship fades away to the horizon. Yet really, they have not gone. All that has happened is that for a time, death has taken them from our sight, and somewhere on the other side, there will be loved ones who have already taken that same journey before them, and who will take up where we leave off gazing towards the horizon and seeing the sailing ship grow in stature as it comes closer, saying, 'Look, here she comes!' ANON.

Two things were said to us after the service which summed up the occasion. Annie's Dad said to Colin 'Your heart must be bursting with pride today' and in spite of the desperate sadness, he was right. We were so proud that our daughter had proved worthy of such a turn out. My Mum's cousin's daughter-in-law, who was there because John wasn't well enough to attend and Isobel was staying with him, had said to Kenny that she had never had the chance to meet Lesley and yet she had walked out feeling as if she had known her all her life. It was such a comfort to me to know that her story had been well told and her life's journey acknowledged.

We had booked the hall at the Hilcroft Hotel where Lesley had her eighteenth birthday party so that anyone who was free could have something to eat and drink after the services and we headed there after Colin and I had stood to thank everyone as they left the crematorium. This meant that the family car was last to arrive and it was immediately obvious that far more people had chosen to come back than we would ever have expected. I was a bit overwhelmed by the noise and the numbers but I knew that I still had to hold things together to thank all of these people who were there to offer their support and to pay respect. The staff members were simply magnificent at dealing with the additional numbers even though they also had a wedding in the hotel that day. Extra tables were organised through in the restaurant and no one was left without food and drink. Colin made a point of going around every single table to thank people for coming, a huge undertaking of which he should feel very proud, and he split himself between the two rooms to make sure no one was missed.

There was such an incredible mix of people present and yet they all had our Lesley in common and it meant there was a real buzz as people were introduced to each other and shared their memories. We were proud to have been able to create such a celebration of Lesley's life though we were beginning to find it all a bit too much. It was with real relief later in the afternoon that we were left with just some of the family to come back to the house and to stop feeling the need for the 'public faces'.

It was only after we were left on our own that I completely broke down for the first time and Colin held me for a very long time while my heart simply broke in two and the reality of our loss kicked in. I sobbed and howled, aware of an animal-like sound that was coming from deep within me but totally out of my control. It was only clinging to Colin that eventually allowed me to calm down though the shaking and shuddering and struggle for breath continued and Colin managed to be the strong one who held me up while despair made me feel like I was drowning. I think I had been so focussed on the funeral and being strong and staying calm that I hadn't allowed myself to really face up to my grief. I had never been a person who cried at all and had developed strong armour over the years to cope with all of the difficult times in Lesley's life by being her rock. Now I felt utterly bereft, lost, diminished as a person and simply broken by the enormity of losing my beloved Lesley.

We felt so alone that night as we faced the reality of having said goodbye to our only child with bleak days lacking meaning and purpose stretching ahead. There had always been the three of us and Lesley had been at the forefront of everything we considered doing. There is a lot of strength in a triangle and we were discovering that a straight line linking two people does not have that same stability and we were going to have to toughen up if we were to be able to go on without becoming bitter or totally withdrawn. The present reality was a lack of balance in the house and Colin and I had never been accustomed to just thinking of ourselves and we found it almost impossible to make the adjustment.

Trying to Find a 'New Normal'

There were still a lot of things to do and I probably found it easier than Colin to cope with focussing on the necessary tasks. Colin decided that he should get back to work to try to establish a 'new normal' and we thought this was the right decision. However, although he could do the work and could cope with going to see customers and have meetings with them, he discovered that bigger team meetings at the office were causing him huge degrees of stress. I think he lost patience with the everyday gripes people made about work or with decisions that had to be made but not followed through. The temptation was to tell people to get into the real world where there were much bigger things to moan about but he knew he couldn't react like that and his stress levels continued to rise and he was frequently exhausted.

I was able to deal with closing Lesley's accounts and subscriptions and getting her name removed so that we didn't keep receiving letters or magazines addressed to her. We had found going to register her death an extremely difficult thing to cope with but the system allowed one phone call that cancelled all of the official things like doctors, hospitals, library, etc. and this reduced the amount of correspondence though there was still a lot to see to. You just shouldn't ever be doing this for your child.

The collection at the funeral had raised £1400 which we split between Disability West Lothian and the Befriender's Scheme and we made sure the cheque was signed by Colin to allow Gift Aid to be claimed on top. When we remade our wills, Lesley had said that she wanted any of her own money to be given to Alzheimer's Scotland and we were glad to honour this wish with £5600 plus Gift Aid. There were other smaller donations in her name to Signpost, the charity I volunteered with and the Speedway Benevolent Fund. Lesley's clothes and her music collection went to charity shops to raise further funds in her name and her upright hairdryer and stand went to Cornerstone so that residents could have a salon-type experience. All in, Lesley was responsible for a five-figure sum being given to various charities and she would have been so proud of this. She had learned to be charitable over the years and when there were appeals made on television she would disappear and return with her phone to send in a text donation so we know that she would take great satisfaction out of giving larger amounts. When we took the cheque to Disability West Lothian, Gordon spoke about the service and how much it had meant to them all. He then showed how much he knew our daughter by telling us that with hundreds of people present to show their respect for her, he had suddenly realised that if she had been able to be present she would have been in the toilet keeping out of the way because she hated to be in the limelight. This was so true and it touched us that they knew her so well.

Family and friends were all given a personal memento and I know that for most of them, this meant a great deal. Frances, our friend and hairdresser was given some computer games for her son Cameron. I had kept pretty little hair clips with little diamond-like stones on them and gave them to Frances feeling they were appropriate though they were not at all valuable. Frances knew the real value of them and later that summer, when she took part in the closing ceremony of the Glasgow Commonwealth Games at Hampden Park – scene of Colin and Lesley's wonderful Hibs League Cup victory - she let us know that the spirit of Lesley would be there because she would be wearing the hair clips for the big occasion. Lynne also quietly told me that she wore the little brooch she had been given when she went to a wedding later in the year. These gestures meant the world to us. Lynnette and Emma were so grateful to have been given mementoes and photographs and also treasured their copies of the order of service from the funeral.

Lesley had been very much a silver jewellery person but she loved to have a two-tone watch with silver and gold so that if she chose to wear any of her few gold items, the watch would still look right. I kept her gold Rennie Mackintosh necklace and bracelet for myself as I only ever wear gold. The necklace is always worn next to my skin under whatever I am wearing every day and it brings me huge comfort. She had a lovely little chain with a jewelled panda on it and Colin hung this from the lamp in his office at home so that it was always right in front of him when he was working. I got key-rings made for both of us with her photograph on them so that everywhere we go we still take her with us. We also kept her charm bracelet because every charm we bought for it had special significance linked to important things in her life and this is greatly treasured but kept safe and never worn.

We tried to do everything that Lesley would have wanted and this had caused me a day of real upset after the funeral when we had to make decisions about Lesley's ashes. I was sure that when we all made our new wills Lesley had said that she just wanted her ashes left at the crematorium and now I didn't want this. Colin said that Lesley wouldn't mind me changing her plans but I felt that this would be disrespectful even though it was upsetting me greatly. However, when I dug out all the things that we had written down which included what Colin and I had chosen as well as Lesley's wishes, to my astonishment, she gave me a 'get-out' clause when I read what she had said. Her instruction was that her ashes were to be left at the crematorium – 'unless her Mum was still around and wanted to do something different!' What a gift she had given me, almost as though she had known.

Initially we thought that the ashes would only be left in one place and we would have chosen the track at the speedway. However, I was speaking to my friend June and mentioned that we thought we could get permission for the speedway track and possibly not be able to do so anywhere else. June's response was that no one needed to know if we were leaving wee amounts in places that meant a lot to us and to Lesley. I could have kissed her for that statement as it opened up a new view of what we could do. Colin and I talked it through carefully and decided that Lesley needed to continue to travel with us and that we would plan where we wanted little amounts of her ashes to be scattered. We had permission from the Monarchs to go to the track on a non-match day and walk around the track ourselves leaving some of her ashes to honour her love of speedway. We decided that the first little journey would be up onto the highest point of the moor where Colin wanted his ashes to be left and where I now wanted mine to be too. We chose a young oak tree and it has become a place where we go often when we need to feel close to Lesley. I tied purple and lilac ribbons on a branch and we feel very close to her when we go there to leave a purple flower for her on important days.

We knew that scattering ashes at Hibs was not encouraged but I bought a tiny little jar that could be in my pocket so that a spoonful of ashes could be left anywhere with utter discretion. Hence, we were able to plan to retrace the footsteps of her life from birth to adulthood and feel that we had given recognition to the places that had been important to her. We also sponsored a heat at the speedway with the message 'Keep Smiling Lesley' and Colin made a donation to the Hibs Fans Trust in her memory, a gesture that was rewarded by the presentation of a framed certificate at the club's training ground with Lesley's photograph attached. Later, when a Fan's Trust was set up for the speedway, we were able to have her name on the 'virtual wall' so that again she could be tangibly remembered and she got a granite stone at the Hibs ground near the gate they entered for matches.

We had a visit from Kenny, Annie, Calum and Lorna one night not long after the funeral and they arrived carrying a large box. We were stunned on opening it to discover that they had spoken to the photographer from the wedding and arranged for three wonderful photographs to be framed in a special three-dimensional frame. The first one showed us arriving, with Lesley and I walking together towards the building; the second was of the three of us at the table after the meal, with Lesley sitting in the middle of us and holding both of our arms; the final one, the last ever photograph of our beloved daughter was of Colin and her on the dance floor just before she had to go and rest. What a gift, what a treasure, we were just speechless. Lesley's happiness radiated from the photographs and captured her joy with both of us and we were so grateful. The little rear hall of our cottage has framed photographs and the framed Hibs certificate and there is real comfort for us in having her smiling at us all over the house. The only room that doesn't have a photograph of her is the bathroom – but we have gulls there in her honour as I'm sure she wouldn't want to be looking out on our ablutions! We truly believe that she is still with us, we just can't see her.

One of the most difficult things we had to do was to go back to the lawyer to cancel the trust and to make new wills that didn't include Lesley. This seemed to be the most final of all of the official things we had to do. When we all went to Edinburgh a few years previously it had been difficult for Lesley because she didn't want to face the fact that we were preparing for a time when she would be without us. Now we found ourselves changing all the plans because it was us who were left without her and it was quite honestly just awful. Everything that we had ever done in life was with Lesley at the forefront and our savings had all been so that she would be secure and able to pay for any additional support she needed to help her to cope alone. The journey home that day was incredibly sad.

Little things happened now and again that lifted us from our heartache. The first day Frances came to cut our hair after Lesley died she asked us if we were aware of Lesley's favourite word – and we didn't know what she was meaning. However as soon as she said 'Absolutely' everything was clear. This – and 'Definitely' – were used so often by Lesley as a way of finding an easy response to questions when she didn't want to get drawn into details. 'Did you have a good holiday Lesley?' 'Absolutely!' 'Did you enjoy your meal Lesley?' 'Absolutely!' 'Are you looking forward to Christmas Lesley?' 'Definitely!' We laughed at the memory – rather tearfully – but we could actually hear her voice in the room.

Colin would switch Lesley's phone on every so often and would discover that she had lots of special occasions stored in the calendar. People's birthdays and anniversaries would flash up showing us again how caring and organised she was. Kenny and Annie got a beautiful Memory Box made for us, white with Lesley's name on it in purple letters. We immediately filled it with precious items and realised that we had to prioritise what should be included as there was not enough space. Then Lesley, one of the Signpost workers, came with a bigger box because she had read about memory boxes and searched for something appropriate in the hope that it would be a help to us. It was amazing to find that both of them were crammed full of things that made us laugh and cry and which summed up our daughter's special life and which we could dip into any time that we were feeling low. There were 'sensible' items like her speedway and football scarves with all her collection of badges but there were daft things included that meant a lot to us and which would make us smile a wee bit in years to come. A mitt to remind us of her special hands, a bed sock to remind us of her cold feet and a pair of her 'lucky knickers' which meant so much to her and reminded us of the unique person she had been.

Never having had a video camera meant that although we had many photographs, we did not have Lesley's voice to listen to. Initially we had been able to phone her mobile and listen to the message she had recorded but one day it had simply disappeared and no one I went to could get it back. Colin had recorded it on his mobile but it was very faint and it meant that if I had a need to hear her voice when Colin wasn't around, I couldn't do it. One of the men at Colin's work took the phone and managed to transfer the recording to the computer so that I could keep it and listen whenever I needed to. Another of the guys also managed to enlarge and print the wonderful photograph of Lesley that Colin had taken with his phone at Hampden when they were at a cup final. These two acts of kindness were treasures for us and we will always be grateful to have them.

We were working in the front garden one day and a lady said hello as she walked past. A short time later we had just finished and were in the kitchen washing our hands when the same lady came to the door carrying flowers. She said that she hadn't been able to attend Lesley's funeral because of work commitments and had wanted to come to see us for a while to express her sympathy. I had to say that I didn't know her and she explained that she only knew Lesley from standing with her at the bus stop on occasion but that Lesley had always been lovely to her and was now greatly missed – and that everyone spoke about how much they missed seeing her lovely smile. It was a simple gesture from a virtual stranger that again showed us how much of an impression Lesley had made on people and stressed the size of the hole she had left behind. She had the smallest feet of any adult I knew but had left behind the biggest footprints ever.

We had entered a world that no one would ever choose to belong to, the world of the bereaved parent. My friend died due to a blood clot when we were in our late teens and her Mum went on to lose not just her husband but one of her other daughters later in life. I had taught a wonderful little boy for three years in my early years of teaching and his parents lost him just after he graduated from university due to cystic fibrosis. As I have said previously, our friends Lynne and Frank lost their son Craig in his twenties in a car accident. A lady we had befriended on holiday in China lost her daughter through illness the year before we lost Lesley. These were all people I considered to be my friends and I was in contact with them over the years of their losses. I thought I had an idea of how their lives had changed due to their loss but the reality is that unless you have lost a child, you have absolutely no concept of how it feels. It is not something you can imagine or link to any other loss. Your child is your future and you should never be packaging up their life and living without them. I had a new respect for the way these friends had conducted themselves after their losses and complete understanding of why they still had bad days where the pain was unbearable and overwhelming.

In the past when I knew of someone about to give birth, I tended to worry until I heard that Mum and baby were both well. Our own experience meant that we knew how bad it felt when things went wrong and we wouldn't wish that on any family. However now we were reacting to every news story on television or in the newspapers where parents had lost a child because we knew the journey they were beginning was the most painful imaginable. Our own rawness was made worse every time we shared the pain of others and we struggled to keep ourselves strong.

I realised that while I had always known that I was Lesley's anchor, in actual fact it turned out that she was mine too. My life was so completely tied to hers that I was finding the absence of her needing me impossible to cope with and the pain really was unbearable. Colin and I were lost. We didn't know how to just please ourselves with the things that had always had to accommodate Lesley's needs and wishes first. I missed all the little things that she needed help with on a daily basis and all the times she checked with me that she was doing the right things and making the right decisions. We had not had the easiest of lives in the past and had needed to cope with many very difficult situations – but if we put Lesley's death on one side of a set of balance scales and then put every other bad experience or worry of the previous 35 years on the other side, the scales would not move by a fraction.

In late summer a letter arrived one day that was difficult to cope with. The final tests from the coroner's office had resulted in them concluding that Lesley's death had been related to epilepsy, even though she hadn't even been having any of the little absences – at least not when she was awake. We were shocked and disbelieving at first and I think our biggest worry was that she might have suffered when her peaceful position and undisturbed bed had comforted us that she had simply slept away. I couldn't stop thinking about it and decided that the only way I could get any peace of mind was to speak to Dr Duncan at the Western General Hospital in Edinburgh. Colin wasn't sure that this was a good idea and wondered if the doctor would even be willing to speak to us but I was driven to make contact.

She was so sorry to hear of Lesley's death and said that she completely understood my need for answers. I knew that she would have to be honest with me and I feared that her words might make things worse – but not knowing was eating me up anyway so I listened to her responses with immense gratitude. She said that she was sure that Lesley would not have suffered at all and that she believed that it would have been like a door opening for her to move to another room. She said that I was right to believe that the fact Lesley was in her usual sleeping position with her covers tucked in and her duvet snug at her neck meant that there had been no trauma, that whatever electrical activity had occurred had coupled with her heart stopping. Probably the kindest thing she said was also the bravest as I might have reacted badly – she said that she hoped I would understand what she meant when she said that it would have been an 'easy' death, one we would all choose if we could, peacefully in our own bed with no pain, suffering or long deterioration. I can't say how much that comforted us and how grateful we were for her being willing to talk to me. She gave me a level of peace and acceptance to be able to move on.

Every so often things happen that feel as though Lesley is giving us little signs that she is with us and looking after us till we are together again – and we cling to the believe that this will happen. At some of our lowest moments we have had an unexpected wildlife encounter, a deer, a red squirrel, a hare – all have appeared as if to lift our spirits and Lesley knew only too well how much we loved animals and birds. Probably the most important for us are seagulls. Colin and I would get very excited by any unusual bird that visited our bird table but the only time Lesley was impressed was if a huge herring gull tried to land on top of the roof of the bird table to steal whatever was on offer. The table wasn't big enough to accommodate the bulk of the gulls and it would shake while the bird tried to reach the food, flapping its wings to keep balanced.

Lesley would shout for us to come quickly to watch it and she would laugh heartily as she watched the antics unfold. When we had listened to the words of 'Into the West' after Jim Brodie's suggestion to use it in the funeral service, we could not believe it when we heard the words *'What can you see on the horizon? Why do the white gulls call? Across the sea, a pale moon rises. The ships have come to carry you home'.* This made us feel that we were being guided to choose things that meant a great deal to the three of us and gave us something to cling on to. As the days and weeks became months we were amazed by the number of times a single white gull would appear unexpectedly at a time when we were coping badly or just needing help to deal with something in everyday life. The gull has become a real symbol for us and we commissioned a local artist to carve us a gull with its wings raised just as the ones landing on our bird table would look. John Donaldson did us proud and Lesley would have loved this fine addition to our living room.

Around the time when we got the gull we had another reminder of how highly thought of our daughter had been to others. We were contacted by Catriona, who had become Lesley's boss at her workplace when Andrew left and she asked if she could come to see us. The reason for her visit turned out to be that we were being invited to attend their annual awards gathering for a very special reason. They also had commissioned something in memory of Lesley – a beautiful award which would be presented annually to a deserving person in Lesley's memory. It was inscribed 'The McRobb Award for Outstanding Disabled Volunteer of the Year' and we were so proud and moved. It was a very emotional presentation and one Lesley would simply not have believed.

Over all the years of my married life I have had small pets – hamsters, guinea pigs, rabbits, a budgie and a chinchilla – then finally, Harvey my giant rabbit. Lesley had accepted rather than doted on my pets and when they died she was upset for me at their loss rather than suffering any grief herself. However even before I bought Harvey Lesley was in love with him. I took her to the pet shop to see him as I was considering getting him but knew that I would need to have a rabbit-hutch that was big enough for him before I could do so. When Colin came home that night she couldn't wait to tell him all about the amazing rabbit we had been to see and told him that he would have to go to the shop at the weekend to see him and that we just had to buy him. Colin and I were amazed at her reaction and from the first moment of him coming into our home she simply adored him. He had an ear that wouldn't go up and he turned out to be blind in one eye – but to Lesley he was the perfect pet. He was laid-back and loved to be petted and she would lie down on the floor to let him jump all over her and then sit happily with him on her knee and enjoy stroking his beautifully soft fur. He was mischievous and would steal fruit from the fruit bowl and nibble the legs of the table – but he was adored. She was so proud of him that I had to take him in to her work for a visit to meet the 'gang' and Emma duly fell in love with him too. He relaxed on her knee as she sat in her wheel-chair throughout our visit and gained himself another fan much to Lesley's delight.

As he got older he became even lazier and just liked to stretch out on the rug in front of the fireplace and 'chill'. We had been told that Harvey would probably only live to around five years old and Colin and I worried about Lesley's reaction to losing him and tried to prepare her for the inevitable. However, Harvey lived to nearly eight years old and didn't die until some weeks after we lost Lesley. We love to think that wherever she is, she is now back having fun with the big, adored bunny and the thought makes us smile. I brought him back from the vet and we buried him in the back garden where she had loved to watch him hop around and our memories of their relationship give us cause to smile.

Also in our back garden, we have a little piece of slate engraved with the message 'Keep Smiling Lesley, we will always love you. 1978 – 2014 EVERGREEN'. The 'evergreen' is doubled edged - Lesley would always be a Hibee and green is their colour but she will also never grow old and will always be young in our memories of her. In actual fact, I think almost everyone thinks of her as a girl, not even as a woman due to her innate naivety and lack of worldliness. All of these little things help us to get through the days when our hearts are breaking and we feel we have honoured her as best we can so that her memory and legacy live on in a great variety of ways.

The First Year

It hasn't been easy to get through the first year without her. We learned that with the big days - the birthdays or anniversaries or Christmas and New Year – the fear of them usually turned out to be worse than the actual days. This doesn't mean that we found them easy; rather we just found strength from somewhere to get us through. We've stopped giving each other birthday or Christmas presents because there is no joy in them when we don't share the moments with our daughter. There were so many ordinary days when for some reason one of us would be utterly raw and heartbroken, crying as badly as in the early days for no apparent reason. We also went through the guilt of realising that we had just laughed at something, then feeling we had no right to ever laugh again without our Lesley.

We returned to the speedway feeling it was the best way to honour Lesley but it was so hard not to have her standing in front of us with Lynnette and celebrating the good wins with a hug and a huge smile. When the team went on to win all of the big titles at the end of the season we truly believed that it was all for Lesley. Even Derek, the captain, told me after they won the first of three titles that they had more to win 'for Lesley' and on the final night when the team had been presented with the League Title he came over to give me a hug and said that she would be dancing 'up there' and sharing the moment – and Colin and I could feel her presence so strongly that night that we believed it. A great many fans gave us hugs on the final night – words weren't necessary, they simply showed that they remembered and that they were thinking of her during the celebrations.

Colin returned to Hibs with me going with him the first time. It was so difficult for him because his Hibee pal is missing now and it will never feel right for him. However, Dave, Karen, Billy, Liz and their families all look after him and understand how much he has lost. He takes Lesley with him in his heart – and there is always a seagull at the stadium. Rod Petrie, the Hibs chairman, had invited Colin to bring me and my brothers to the first match of the new season as his guests but Colin couldn't face it so we thanked him but turned down his kind invitation. Then just before Christmas Rod got back in touch and said that he would love us all to come to the Rangers game, remembering that my brothers and I were all Rangers fans. We accepted gratefully, enjoyed pre-and post-match hospitality in the directors' box and with Hibs thrashing Rangers it felt as though Lesley was there too, not just her scarf on my knee. When we were speaking with Rod in the Director's Lounge before the match we thanked him again and he said it was his privilege because Lesley had been a well-known face at Hibs and at other stadiums. These kinds of experiences are always bitter-sweet and difficult to cope with but they mean so much.

By the August of that first year, Colin was finding work increasingly difficult to cope with and he worried that it was all getting on top of him. He attended a management meeting at the office one day and was very unhappy about some of the decisions which he didn't feel were right. He had phoned me while he had his lunch and talked about feeling frustrated and compromised but by the time he had voiced his thoughts he felt calmer. However, on returning for the afternoon session a compromise too far was expected and he simply said that he couldn't agree and wasn't willing to go along with it. He closed his computer, left the office and came home to tell me that he just couldn't do it anymore and that he felt he had to leave.

At this time, I was finding it difficult just to focus on doing the minutes for a couple of hours at Signpost board meetings so I understood how hard it was for him to cope with long meetings where big issues had to be handled. His relief was profound when I said that he had to do what was right for him and that I was totally behind his decision. He cried for a while and then slept for hours and then we discussed how to move forward. He made an appointment to talk to his doctor and ended up being signed off work while he worked his notice. He did go back to the office and worked with Alan, his boss, to leave everything in as good a state as possible and he has been happy to help out occasionally since.

However, it was the right move for him as his own weakened general health wouldn't have sustained the stress he was under.

Sadly, I think that he went backwards over the first winter and I should probably have pushed him to do more. We went on holiday rather unsuccessfully and after that experience Colin simply didn't want to do anything social. Having to make small talk with strangers proved much more difficult than we could have imagined – particularly if they asked if we had any family. How do you answer without making them feel uncomfortable? We also found that there was no balance with just the two of us and the loss of Lesley was much more difficult to bear. It was always 'The Three Musketeers on Tour' so none of it felt right. It was a huge relief for both of us to get back home.

I had begun to volunteer with MacMillan doing risk assessment home visits for the Helping Matters volunteer scheme and this gave me a new focus on top of my Signpost work. I could make myself put my armour on to manage and even if I was a bit wrung out afterwards, I could cope with the visits, meetings and training days related to my volunteering. However, by the end of October there was no speedway to go to and Colin didn't want to go out anywhere, not even for a lunch. We both had a fear of being 'wet blankets' and other than having a few couples that we visited for an afternoon or them coming to us, we withdrew socially. It wasn't that we were consciously being miserable but it was just easier to be ourselves in our own house where we most felt that we had Lesley with us.

In November, we were facing Lesley's birthday without her for the first time and it was such a comfort to have people who got in touch with us, visited or sent flowers. The very worst thing for us to cope with was the thought of Lesley being forgotten so tangible reminders that she was still in other people's thoughts really were necessary to help us. Her friends Lynnette and Emma had been stars during all the months since Lesley's death and had continued to phone, text and ask me to meet up with them for coffees. Lynnette had come to terms with visiting the house without Lesley being there and over the winter she took on the role of being our 'minder' checking with us once a week that we were doing all right. Emma bought a green phone and would paint her nails green in honour of Lesley's love of Hibs. These girls missed Lesley so much and knew how broken we were. They enjoyed sharing their memories of her and there would be laughter and tears when we met up.

Although there were people who didn't keep in touch who might have been expected to, there were others who were only on the fringes of our lives who kept in contact and made us feel stronger by their kindness. It was proving to be a much more difficult journey to make than we could ever have imagined so anything that helped a bit was gratefully embraced. I thought that when the speedway season started again in March it would help us to consider going out more. It was quite a shock for me to find that I was the one who couldn't cope on the first couple of nights. On the opening night of the season Lesley and I would always go to buy year badges for our scarves, a new Monarchs key-ring for Lesley and a new team photograph for the programme holder. On the first night, I just didn't know what to do. Should I buy a badge for Lesley's scarf as well as mine, should I leave it as it had been when she last wore it or should I just stop having one on mine too? I agonised so much over what to do that I was totally wound up by the time the meeting started and then I missed Lesley standing in front of me even more than the previous season. The noise and the crowds were beyond dealing with and we ended up leaving early because I was struggling to stop myself breaking down completely – it just felt so wrong. The following week wasn't much better but then I got to grips with putting my face on and trying to focus on the racing. It proved though that we really had gone backwards over the winter months and we had to be more positive.

We had decided that we should try again to go on holiday and that it might be best to do something that was unlike anything we had done as a threesome. With this in mind we booked a rail journey to Puglia in Italy where we were to be staying in one of the Trulli houses. Colin loved rail travel and we both thought the area looked fascinating and the unusual accommodation meant that we wouldn't just be spending our time with lots of other people in a hotel; we would have our own space when we needed it.

We were going in April and booked to travel to London by train the day before, staying overnight to be ready for the early morning departure. Everything was well planned and Kenny gave us a lift to our local station for us to go to Edinburgh to board the London train. We were both fine that morning and looking forward to the journey and we were quite excited about travelling in a first-class compartment for the first time, a little treat to make the first part of the journey more enjoyable. We had individual seats facing each other over a table and were kept topped up with water, coffee, biscuits and sandwiches. I noticed after a couple of hours that Colin had become very quiet but I wasn't aware of how bad he was feeling until we were close to London. He wasn't really answering me and was looking very grey and drawn but wouldn't say what was wrong.

When we arrived at King's Cross Station we were faced with the busy metropolis of London and that seemed to be the last straw for Colin. Instead of getting a buzz out of being in the capital, he totally withdrew as we headed to our overnight accommodation. By the time we got to our room he looked awful and said that he had to go to bed. He slept for a few hours but when he woke up he was no better and said he wanted to go home, the holiday was off because he simply couldn't face it. I was shocked and said that we couldn't possibly go back home that night, thinking that he would be fine in the morning. I couldn't get him to tell me what was wrong, all he could say was that it was all wrong and he needed to go home. The more I tried to get him to talk the more of a panic he was getting into and he seemed to be struggling just to breath. He wouldn't eat or drink, in fact he didn't even take his kidney medications, and he ended up getting back into bed and going to sleep.

I lay awake all night and early in the morning I woke him to see if he was feeling better. Sadly, he wasn't and I had to phone to say that we would not be joining the trip. Colin still wouldn't – or couldn't – eat or drink and I was worried about the effects this would be having on his kidneys. The only thing he could tell me afterwards was that he suddenly realised that we might be spending two days travelling with people sitting beside us who wanted to talk all the time – and this had sent him into total panic and he felt everything was closing in on him. He said that even trying to talk to me felt impossible. He got dressed without even getting washed or shaved and said that we had to get out of the 'prison cell' of a room so that we could get home. We checked out and made our way back to King's Cross with Colin stooped and shuffling and totally silent. I got him a seat at the station and went to find out when we could get a train home. We were lucky and managed to get booked on the 9.00 a.m. train so only had about an hour to wait. It was heart-breaking to see Colin looking so ill and he spent almost the entire journey asleep.

The train steward kept offering me food or drinks for Colin obviously very concerned and I could only say that he was feeling ill and just needed to sleep. I sent a text to Kenny to see if he happened to be free to pick us up at the station and thankfully he changed his own plans to meet us with Annie. They were obviously shocked when we got off and they saw the 'poor old man' who had come back with me. When they brought us home Colin just went straight to bed and again slept for hours. Kenny and Annie stayed with me for a while to make sure that I was all right – even if devastated by the events of the last 24 hours. Thankfully when Colin woke up that night he was able to have a sandwich with a cup of tea and to take his tablets – and to begin to talk. Lots of his feelings came out over the next couple of days and he admitted that he just wasn't managing to handle his grief or deal with the loss of our Lesley and he admitted that he needed help. He had lots of anger and resentment inside that was bottled up and it was stopping him from moving on.

We had to face that we weren't going to be able to help each other if one of us was stuck in a place that the other one couldn't reach and we made an appointment for Colin to see a counsellor. This proved to be of benefit because it allowed him to talk out all of the things that he thought and felt and to be reassured that everything he mentioned was perfectly normal and that lots of people in our situation had said exactly the same things. He had been judging himself against me and he knew that I didn't have any anger so he thought he was in the wrong. Just talking it all out helped and he added a few more sessions with the counsellor over the next couple of months until he felt stronger and calmer. We both admitted that we needed to find a new approach to life and that we couldn't simply give in as that would have been no tribute to Lesley who had always been expected to make the best of difficult times. However, in spite of her needs and limitations I think she had been the glue in our family life and we were left feeling completely fractured without her by our sides.

If we asked Lesley what she loved most about me, it was that I was her best friend and she was so glad that I was always there for her. I know now that she was always there for me too and I have lost my best friend, the daughter that I knew inside out and it is a loss that just cannot be made up for in any way. If we asked her what she loved most about her Dad she would instantly say that Colin made her laugh – and that was often when life was really tough, when Colin's humour lightened her dark times. Now Colin feels guilty if his innate sense of humour bubbles to the surface because the person he most liked to impress with his daft jokes and quick one-liners is no longer there. He cracks a joke and then feels bad about it because his wee Hibee pal isn't there to share the laughter and that's so sad. However, we do strive to cope and we know that we have to go on without her somehow.

As the first months became the first year we began to try to do more than just go out for walks. We would sometimes get the bus into Glasgow or Edinburgh and have a coffee and a wander around on mid-week days when streets were quiet. Occasionally we went to the cinema and even had lunch out a couple of times which was all heading in a more positive direction. Colin suggested booking another holiday but I was scared of trying anything that wouldn't work out thus setting us further back than ever. We had always gone up to Aviemore for an overnight every year to visit Colin's adopted reindeer on Cairngorm and I wondered if this might be a good idea so I found a little cabin where we could be self-catering and only eat out if we really wanted to, not because we had to. We could do as much or as little as we felt like and the car would be there if we did need to come home before the six days was up. Thankfully it worked quite well – and if I'm honest, Colin was more relaxed than I was. I think I was waiting for it to go badly wrong and was so glad that it didn't even on days where things were a wee bit shaky. As I write this we are planning a week later in the year in a little cottage in Wales and hopefully that will work too and let us know that we are doing better at coping.

I don't know how to end the story which I did say at the beginning would not be in a happy way. I'm quite worried about coming to the end because the writing has given me a sense of purpose and I will need to find other ways of dealing with my thoughts and emotions. Lesley would be stunned if she could see how often her Mum, who never cried, quietly weeps and some days my crying can still be heart-rending sobs. Colin and I have worked very hard at trying to be 'together' in how we face things and deal with them and although we may grieve in different ways, we are so lucky to have each other to love and to hold on to in the blackest moments. However, life is really tough now and we do need to focus on keeping our public faces in place as much as we possibly can.

I find that I often recall the little prayer Lesley said as a child when we settled her down at night. We would tuck her up in bed and read her a story. Then I taught her to say the little prayer that many of you will have repeated in your childhood. It should say:

Now I lay me down to sleep I pray the Lord my soul to keep; If I should die before I wake I pray the Lord my soul to take.

However, with all the worries in her first year with operations and illness I hated the final words and changed them for Lesley. She learned to say:

Now I lay me down to sleep I pray the Lord my soul to keep; Guard and keep me through the night and wake me with the morning light.

She would finish by saying: *God bless Mum and Dad and all the people I love and make me a good girl. Amen*

Now these words haunt me. What drove me to change them? I had been sure before Lesley was born that there was something wrong. I had also said to Colin that I didn't think she would live into old age though I had never expected that we would lose her at only thirty-five. Did I sub-consciously know that there would come a morning when she wouldn't wake and feel driven to ask for the morning light always to wake her? I just know how much I believe that her spirit is still with us every day, guiding us and trying to give us strength. There has never been a single day that we didn't mention her since we lost her. We know how she would have reacted to funny things and we quote her often. I can't look at a menu without choosing what she would have had. We hear songs that were her favourites and they make us smile or cry depending on how we are feeling. We 'see' her sitting, smiling and loving us in our home and we feel her presence everywhere we go.

If you have read my daughter's story and you know people in your own circle who have lost their child, please try to be there for them. Don't just think it's for the first few weeks – these days may be difficult but things get worse after the initial numbness wears off and you are left to try to live a life you didn't ever choose. Pop in for a visit, phone them and let them talk about their loved one. Forgive their tears and don't be embarrassed if they break down, it's not your fault and they need to be able to express how they feel and know that other people are still thinking about their child. Don't cross the road rather than meet a bereft parent, don't pretend everything is fine and ignore the whole situation, just try to acknowledge the loss in words or by a touch on the arm or even just a kindly glance. Actually, we both think that a hug is the best thing of all. Don't use the excuse of not knowing what to say to avoid saying anything. Don't tell them that time will help – so far, it hasn't for us at all and more than a year down the line I need Lesley to be here more than I did at the beginning of the grieving. Don't say that life goes on – they know that, but it isn't the life they thought they had and nothing prepared them for what they are now living through. There is no magic wand, no quick fix, no way to repair a broken heart but the parents need to know that you are thinking of them and that their child, who should still have been with them, has not been forgotten.

So, are we coping without our Lesley? The short answer is, not really. We try to have public faces but we're both different people now and even though more than a year has passed we still have to work hard at finding a way forward. It all just hurts so much and our lives are empty, lacking purpose and lacking joy. I can't put into words how much we miss the cuddles we got every day, the thanks for the smallest of things and the telling us how much she loved us. I'm not ashamed of the tears that I shed regularly – our daughter is worthy of them. I feel diminished as a person and even though I have things I do that contribute in society, I still feel cut adrift, rudderless and my life lacks meaning without my Lesley. I've lost the calm strength and courage that I thought was part and parcel of me – but was obviously so linked to Lesley that she took it with her when she went. I know that I was her Mum, her carer, her advisor, her confidante and her best friend and losing all of this leaves a hole that cannot be filled.

For Colin, it is coping with anger that is making life most difficult and at times he tends to feel that everything is wrong which causes him to over-react to little things that really shouldn't matter. He told me recently that it feels as though his grief is like a strong elastic band around his waist anchored to the post that was his life before losing Lesley. Just as he feels he has managed to move forward a little bit the elastic becomes too strong for him and it pulls him back violently – and every time he is pulled back he is actually further back than where he started from. He knows he needs to find a way of cutting the elastic but I think he feels that would be like leaving Lesley behind which of course we'll never do. The sense of humour that he and Lesley shared is now such a loss to him and the everyday fun that was part and parcel of our family life has just disappeared. He is now focussing on getting through one day at a time without thinking ahead and if that one day is reasonably all right, then he can reassure himself that he is learning to cope no matter how little progress he feels he is making.

I read a line in a novel recently that said the quality that sets us apart from other animals is Hope, the middle name I gave my baby thirty-five and a half years before we lost her. Maybe I always knew that this was what would get us all through the difficult times and would make us strive to be the best we could be. Maybe I was always aware deep inside that Lesley's life wouldn't be easy, that she would have more trials to face than anyone else I have ever known but that Hope would keep us reaching for the stars and living our dreams. Maybe I already knew that her life would not last as long as we might want her and need her to be with us but that Hope would keep us focussed on a bright tomorrow even in the darkest nights.

Now Hope is still a focus for us and I believe she left it with us to help us to cope without her. We Hope that Lesley would be proud of us and know that we always did our best for her and will continue to try to do so in her honour. We Hope that she knows how much of a mark she left behind in this world and realises how much she was loved and valued and admired and how greatly she is missed. We Hope that where she is now she is happy, that she already knows what we need to believe – that we will be together again one day, the Three Musketeers once more. We Hope that where she is time is nothing, that she has no long days of waiting, like we do, and that she is well and strong and smiling, that the sun always glints on her curls and sparkles in her eyes.

When the first anniversary of Lesley's death came around we were amazed by the number of people who remembered and got in touch to show they cared. We had visits, phone calls, e-mails, texts, cards and flowers and we so appreciated all of it. These people have no idea how much they helped us, Colin particularly. It allowed him to believe that it wasn't only us who were missing her and thinking of her and revisiting our memories of her. Hopefully it will eventually help him to move on from the anger and bitterness that holds him back.

When the flowers faded and needed to be thrown out, Colin was taking some of them to the bin but a gust of wind blew the petals off as soon as he stepped outside. Initially he felt upset as he saw the petals fly into the air and then he came back in to tell me what had happened. He said that in his head he had been saying thank you again to the people who had shown they remembered, to those who had helped us to get through this first dark year without our child. As the wind whipped up he realised that every petal was a memory of the life of a truly remarkable, very special, dearly loved and much missed daughter – our Lovely Lesley.

Lesley, we will always love you. Thank you for being our daughter – it is an honour to have been your parents.

Night, night; love you lots; see you in the morning. xxx

In Closing

I hope you'll permit me a bit of sentimentality by sharing some of the poems I have written during the dark nights of missing my Lesley, my daughter and best friend.

One Day More

If we had one day more, we'd hug you tight and then
We'd see your smile and smell your hair and hold your hand again.
We need to know you're well, that you're happy where you are
We miss you more than words can say - you're now our distant star.
You left us without warning - we didn't know you'd gone
You'd said good night, you loved us lots, but you'd left before the morn.
You were our only child and we loved you from the start
Your life was never easy but you had the bravest heart.
You faced your trials with courage, touched people where you went
But life took its toll and drained you, your energy was spent.
Our hearts are broken now and every day's an effort
But you send us special little signs to show us your support.
A white feather or a deer, a gull screeching in the sky
We thank you and we're grateful but they often make us cry.
We just love you and we miss you, no one can take your place
If only we could see you, touch your hand or stroke your face
Our lives are now so empty and our hearts are very sore
If a miracle was offered we'd just ask for one day more.

Say Her Name

Don't let us think she's forgotten,
That it's only us who care
We look at the empty space in our home
And know she should still be there.

Allow us to talk, forgive us our tears
Share your memories with us too
She should still be here, she went much too soon
There was so much more left to do.

We lost our only daughter
It's a pain we're scarce able to bear
We try to be strong, put brave faces in place
But please let us know that you care.

It's a pain no parent should suffer
It's a loss too big to ignore
There isn't a way to recover
Life just can't go on like before

Say her name to honour her memory
Cry a tear - she deserves quite a few
Say her name with a smile for days gone by
Show she's missed by us –and by you

Send me a rainbow

Whenever I see a rainbow
I always think of you
The colours give a sign of hope
To help me muddle through

The warmth of red and orange
Remind me of your love
The brightest blue seems heaven sent
A message from you above

The green and yellow signs of spring
To move us from regret
The purple shades, your favourites
The colours we won't forget

The soaring arc high in the sky
Linking heaven with earth below
This sign of hope in darkest days
The beautiful rainbow

When dark clouds overpower me
And your loss is too great to bear
A rainbow in the brightening sky
Gives a sign that you're still there

There's no word for what we are now

There's no word for what we are now
There's no word that can explain
We've lost our only child you see
All we feel is loss and pain

Dead parents leave an orphan,
A lost husband a widow will make
But there's no word for what we are now
Even though our poor hearts break

We're bereft and so diminished
We're empty, lost and alone
Our only child was taken too soon
And we don't know how to go on

In earlier days we were parents
A loving family of three
But now we feel we are nothing
There's only my husband and me

We're living on precious memories
They keep us going when life is too tough
But we long for our special daughter
And oh, how we both miss her love

There's no word for what we are now.

What We Miss Most

It's the little things we both miss most that nothing can replace
And we know that this will ever be, no one can take your place
Your hair, fresh washed, your own perfume, your simple sense of style
It's the cuddles that you gave us and the twinkle in your smile

It's your gentle hand on Dad's left leg when tension makes it shake
The sound of music in your room from the minute that you wake
It's your helping in the kitchen and your banter in the car
Shopping trips with some hot chocolate, a scone, a cup of char

Your caring ways; your loyalty; your loving and your giving
Your gratefulness, your innocence, your simple joy of living
It's the three of us together sharing stories, cracking jokes
Seeing all that this world offers, meeting lots of lovely folks

Our hearts are sore with loss now; it's a pain beyond compare
We grieve and mourn, we cry out loud because you aren't there
Our memories sustain us, we treasure them anew
Don't ask us what we miss the most, we're simply missing you

Where Are You?

Where are you now we've lost you, and can't hold you anymore?
When we sense you, but can't see you and our hearts are very sore
We really need to touch your face and hold your hand again
But you send us little signs of hope to help us bear our pain
You're the deer next to the road-side, the buzzard soaring high
The snowdrop in the winter and the summer butterfly
You're the rainbow when a storm has passed, or the early morning dew
When we hear a sea-bird calling we know it's really you
You're the gentle cooling breeze when days warm up in spring
The sparkle of a snowflake or a blackbird's glossy wing
You're the brightest star above us in the midnight winter sky
The coral in the sea depths or the dolphins leaping high
You're the winning goal in football to help Hibs win the cup
The five–one at the speedway when the final tapes go up
You're the top note of the music or the best part of a meal
The footsteps on the dancefloor for a lively Scottish reel
You're the distant shores we travelled to, the mountains and the seas
The elephants, koalas and orang utans in trees

Where are you when we need you, when our hearts are full of care?
We don't need to ask the question for we know you're everywhere.

An Angel on my Shoulder

There's an angel on my shoulder everywhere I go
She's been there for some time now and I really need her so
When I lost my lovely daughter and I thought my heart would break
The angel came and took my hand to soothe the awful ache
Sometimes I'll see a rainbow or a star up in the sky
Or maybe a black rabbit or a seagull flying high
There might be a white feather before me on the ground
Or comfort in the darkness when my pain's the only sound
I know my daughter's with me when I'm feeling really sad
She sends some lovely memories to help me and her Dad
We're trying to be brave though loss has made us feel much older
But she's helped us both by sending me an angel for my shoulder.